PENGUIN BOOKS

LOOKING BEYOND ~~THE IVY~~ LEAGUE

LOREN POPE, a Was~~hington news~~paperman who had led the fight for be~~tter schools in~~ rural Loudoun County, Virginia, first start~~ed writing~~ a column about education for the Gannett Newspapers in 1952, which led to the education editorship of the *New York Times* during the height of the college-going chaos of the late 1950s. Then, and later as a top administrator of what is now Oakland University in Michigan, he became deeply concerned with the lack of consumer information on colleges, and the heavy dropout, transfer, and failure rates resulting from uninformed choices. This concern was triggered by the poor advice he got for his own son from friends in the then Office of Education.

In 1965, he opened the College Placement Bureau in Washington to help families make informed, fruitful choices. Out of his reporting and research came a book, *The Right College: How to Get In, Stay In, Get Back In* (Macmillan, 1970), and several magazine articles, including the nationally syndicated "Twenty Myths That Can Jinx Your College Choice," first published in the *Washington Post Magazine. Reader's Digest* has sold half a million reprints of its condensation, titled "Facts to Know in Picking a College."

Pope has been a contributor to professional journals and a speaker at meetings of the National Association of College Admissions Counselors. He has also appeared on radio and television. He lives in Alexandria, Virginia.

LOOKING BEYOND THE
IVY LEAGUE

FINDING THE COLLEGE THAT'S RIGHT FOR YOU

NEW REVISED EDITION

Loren Pope

PENGUIN BOOKS

PENGUIN BOOKS

Published by the Penguin Group

Penguin Group (USA) Inc., 375 Hudson Street, New York, New York 10014, U.S.A.
Penguin Group (Canada), 90 Eglinton Avenue East, Suite 700, Toronto, Ontario,
Canada M4P 2Y3 (a division of Pearson Penguin Canada Inc.)
Penguin Books Ltd, 80 Strand, London WC2R 0RL, England
Penguin Ireland, 25 St Stephen's Green, Dublin 2, Ireland
(a division of Penguin Books Ltd)
Penguin Group (Australia), 250 Camberwell Road, Camberwell, Victoria 3124,
Australia (a division of Pearson Australia Group Pty Ltd)
Penguin Books India Pvt Ltd, 11 Community Centre, Panchsheel Park,
New Delhi – 110 017, India
Penguin Group (NZ), 67 Apollo Drive, Rosedale, North Shore 0632, New Zealand
(a division of Pearson New Zealand Ltd.)
Penguin Books (South Africa) (Pty) Ltd, 24 Sturdee Avenue,
Rosebank, Johannesburg 2196, South Africa

Penguin Books Ltd, Registered Offices:
80 Strand, London WC2R 0RL, England

First published in Penguin Books 1990
Revised and updated edition published 1995
This second revised and updated edition published 2007

3   5   7   9   10   8   6   4   2

Copyright © Loren Pope, 1990, 1995, 2007
All rights reserved

LIBRARY OF CONGRESS CATALOGING IN PUBLICATION DATA
Pope, Loren.
Looking beyond the Ivy League : finding the college that's right for you /
Loren Pope.—New rev. ed.
p. cm.
Includes index.
ISBN 978-0-14-311282-2
1. College choice—United States. 2. Universities and colleges—United States—
Evaluation. I. Title.
LB2350.5.P67   2007
378.1'0560973—dc22   2007015550

Printed in the United States of America
Designed by Sabrina Bowers

To Ann Rittenberg, my literary agent and former client (good small college, Eckerd), who now has Ivies working for her. She got me off dead center to write about my mission: to change the way people think about colleges. Her keen judgment has made my work popular and helpful to more people.

Contents

CONTENTS

Preface: Why a Second Edition

The colleges themselves have not changed since the first edition of this book came out in 1990. Colleges rarely do, but perceptions of the top universities should—and do. Two prestigious Ivy scholars, from Princeton and Harvard, have said, as detailed elsewhere in the book, that liberal education doesn't exist in the research universities, and that they are failing the nation.

These exposés are overdue; the feverish struggle to get into one of the elite universities is growing worse year by year. Getting into a name college is probably the number-one family anxiety, and it is a foolish pursuit. There are hundreds of good small colleges that want students and that will do more than the elites to develop teenagers into good leaders and citizens. The universities are, and have been for decades, guilty of false and misleading advertising; the testimony of Princeton's Dr. Stanley N. Katz and Harvard's former dean, Dr. Harry Lewis, indicates that they are harming youths.

I hope this book makes even more forceful the truth that the key to the good life is choosing a college for the help it will give you in becoming a good and moral citizen.

Acknowledgments

Besides the debt I owe to students, faculty, and others at the colleges for my enlightenment, two incomparably able mothers are the ones who have done the work that has freed countless families from the college admissions frenzy. One is Virginia Buege, executive director of the Colleges That Change Lives Web site and the one who conceived the idea for and has flawlessly coordinated the CTCL tours since 1998. These tours have visited hundreds of cities at the requests of high school counselors and have changed the way many thousands of families think about colleges.

The other is Martha (Marty) O'Connell, who resigned from what I assume was a six-figure income job as vice president for enrollment and financial aid at McDaniel College to become a missionary for CTCL. McDaniel's president, Dr. Joan Foley, said of Marty, "Most people are easily replaced; Marty is irreplaceable." Out of the fullness of her experience, she has updated and largely rewritten the chapter on financial aid.

Introduction

This book of mine, which will help you fulfill your college command—open sesame!—is a lot more than a magic phrase. It brings an unmatched expertise—half a century of investigating and writing about colleges, of being education editor of the *New York Times*, of being a college official, and of counseling students and their parents on good educational goals—to helping you open the door to the right college.

Opening this door may not be done easily, much less with a single command, but the task will be exciting and successful, and will reward you for a lifetime. The enlightenment and guidance herein will not only give you confidence, but guide you to an experience no Ivy or Ivy clone can match. It will also free you from the nervous collapse suffered by untold scores of thousands each year. Guaranteed.

Long ago, I was frustrated as a parent to learn that while there was plenty of objective data—much of it of little value—there were few guiding clues for picking good colleges, a conviction later reinforced when I became an education writer and editor.

Today the college search has become a national frenzy, the family's principal worry, but you don't have to be one of the afflicted. The criteria for most people are status and prestige, meaning selectivity. Decades ago, in a static establishment society where connections counted, these criteria had market value. In today's and tomorrow's pioneering society of new careers, they are and will be dross. The rewards are going to the risk takers who can *use* knowledge, not those with the greatest store of it—people who can see and make connections, people of character.

Status and prestige have long failed the test of preparation for life. When I started an education column for the Gannett Newspapers in 1952, only four in ten freshmen were on the same campuses four years later. The most recent study found the figure had shrunk to three in ten.

Later, as education editor of the *New York Times* at the crest of the college hysteria, and still later as a top administrator of what is now Oakland University in Michigan, I developed a plan for consumer research on colleges to help people make more fruitful choices by providing the vital information that the directories didn't and don't give. I opened the College Placement Bureau in Washington, D.C., in 1965 to counsel students and parents and help them choose colleges most likely to have a beneficial impact. Often those schools have been ones the parents had never heard of. Indeed, many parents, alums of famous schools, have written to me that they wish they'd had experiences as good as their children had. Occasionally they've also expressed pleasure about how their children's preparation had made easy the work in graduate or professional school. In fact, many no-name but catalytic colleges have far higher graduate and professional school acceptance rates than big and well-known schools. One reason is that seniors in the good small colleges score higher on the graduate tests than those at most Ivies.

For many years I've been in the company of the best minds in education who have said to a nonlistening world that the small college dedicated to a liberal education is not just the wisest and best but also the most practical in a world in which most of tomorrow's jobs don't even exist yet. It is the truth.

The future specialists—the physicians, artists, newspaper reporters, or engineers—can specialize later, after they've had exposure to ideas that will make them better specialists. They must realize that they are human beings first, involved in mankind, as John Donne said. John Stuart Mill put it approximately this way: If you make a man a reasonable and sensible man, he will make himself a reasonable and sensible doctor or philosopher or plumber. Graduate and professional schools don't liberate; they only train specialists.

When Thomas Jefferson, himself the founder of a university, said there cannot be a democracy without an educated public, he meant an informed, moral, and enlightened public, not a vocationally or professionally trained one. The big universities have no mission to produce informed, moral, and enlightened citizens. That role has been left completely to the good four-year liberal arts colleges.

Any doubt about the fact that Mammon, not the students, is the god the universities serve was erased in 2005 by a distinguished Ivy savant, Dr. Stanley N. Katz, the director of Princeton University's Center for Arts and Cultural Policy Studies, president emeritus of the American Council of Learned Societies, and a Harvard alumnus as well as a former faculty member. Dr. Katz said, "Liberal education in the research universities is a project in ruins." The neglect is so bad, in fact, that it threatens "the vitality" of our democracy. Liberal education, he said, is not on the universities' agenda. Their specialist scholars wouldn't be much good at liberal education anyway; "values make them uncomfortable." There's not much hope of change either, he said; the universities' priorities "have been reversed."

A prime example is Johns Hopkins University. With about 4,417 students, the institution takes in $150 million or so in tuition, but it rakes in over $664 billion in research income. You don't have to be a churchgoer to know that where thy treasure is, there is thy heart also.

In other words, you will be cheated out of your birthright of an education at the big university, but, as Dr. Katz said, "Liberal education is alive and well at the four-year undergraduate colleges."

The central message of this book is that while most college choices are so foolishly made that most students eventually forsake or flunk out of them, almost any youth has an array of colleges to choose from that will make a lifelong difference. And prestige has very little to do with it. What counts is not the label but the quality of the experience in developing the potential of the youth into the power of an adult. Furthermore, many of these colleges are looking for you; they want you.

What I hope this book and its sibling, *Colleges That Change Lives*, will do is free parents and their sons and daughters from the barren idolatry to the false gods of name and size and prestige. I hope it will help them identify the real virtues of mental and moral growth so they can make their most important investment give them a lifetime of satisfaction. I think I have clearly marked the path through the thicket of irrelevancies, the perils, and the tempting snares to the castle atop the hill. The reader can set out with confidence.

LOOKING BEYOND THE
IVY LEAGUE

CHAPTER 1

Twenty-one Myths That Can Jinx Your College Choice

YEAR AFTER YEAR AFTER YEAR, they go on jinxing.

A house may be the costliest thing most families buy, but college—which is second—is far more important, because that investment affects their teenager's future. The four college years are the last important developmental period of youth, and what happens then has substantial, life-long consequences. The youth can be awakened to develop himself, his talents and his values. Or he can plod through largely untouched and unenlightened, bored and frustrated, leading him to transfer, drop out, or flunk out. Unbelievable as it may seem, nearly 70 percent of all students suffer one of these unhappy fates.

Even aside from such considerations as the credentials and the fun and status of going to college, the quality of the experience can make such a difference in a person's life that where he goes is more important than whether he goes. (He *could* educate himself on his own in the library.) The magic is in the moral and intellectual torque the college exerts, not in the name, however hallowed it may be. And a continuing irony of the annual college search is that in our vastly over-built education establishment, many good colleges are eager to be found.

But how do intelligent parents and students, confronted with an array of two thousand possible choices, mostly shoddy or unsuitable, arrive at their decisions in making this critical and costly purchase? Do they do some probing consumer research? Do they ask for performance data? Do they sample and test the merchandise? No. And unfortunately there is no consumer research available to the public in this vital field. The reports of accrediting teams are more jealously guarded than any defense secret. There is much objective data in directories but few guiding clues to reveal the many obvious or subtle differences in ambience, values, or character among colleges of the same level of rigor, and none of the long-term performance of their products. No one would pick a wife or a husband or even buy a house or a car with so little information.

The result is that the American family relies chiefly on the pig-in-a-poke method of college selection, based on twenty-one myths that profoundly influence millions of unfortunate, and some fortunate, college choices. On the whole it is such bad consumerism that only 30 to 40 percent of any fall's freshman class will still be in the same colleges four years later. These myths constitute a body of dogma accepted as gospel by the able and mediocre student alike. Here they are, with the lowdown on each.

MYTH ONE: *An Ivy League* school will absolutely guarantee the rich, full, and successful life.*

Looking in the rear-view mirror is what keeps this one alive. For decades I've been saying an "Ivy League education" is an oxymoron and a sham. Now an eminent Princeton scholar and a former Harvard dean not only agree with me, but do me several better. Perhaps people will listen. The Princeton scholar is Dr. Stanley N. Katz, president emeritus of the American Council of Learned Societies a Harvard alum and former faculty member. He says in the April 1, 2005, *Chronicle of Higher Education* that "liberal education in the research universities is a project in ruins." He sees no hope of change, and that those specialized scholars at big universities wouldn't be much good at liberal education anyway. What's more, the universities are uncomfortable with values, which are central to the good small college.

But in the good small college, liberal education is "alive and well."

Harvard's Dr. Harry Lewis, a faculty member for more than thirty years and its dean for eight, has written a book, *Excellence without a Soul: How a Great University Forgot Education*, in which he details his school's failings and their causes. In the chapter "H Is for Harvard and Hypocrisy" he says that the purpose of education is to help teenagers find themselves and to make moral adults of them, and that Harvard and its clones fail abysmally.

---

* The eight universities constituting the Ivy League are Brown, Columbia, Cornell, Dartmouth (which calls itself a college), Harvard, Pennsylvania, Princeton, and Yale. The Little Ivies are Amherst, Wesleyan, and Williams.

The corporate downsizing upheaval in the early 1990s had already demolished the "guarantee" part of the myth. In a two-page spread titled "The Humbling of the Harvard Man" in the March 2, 1994, Sunday business section of the *New York Times*, fully a quarter of Harvard alumni reported at the thirty-fifth anniversary of the class of 1958 that they were out of work, looking for work, or on welfare. The autobiographical sketches they submitted, said author and Yale professor Eric Segal, "did not radiate with expressions of success and optimism. Quite the contrary, they seemed like a litany of loss and disillusion." Senator John D. Rockefeller added, "The layoffs of managers and skilled technical people at Xerox or IBM or AT&T do not discriminate between the graduates of Harvard and some lesser school. And when the layoffs come we are not prepared for non-success. We don't know how to deal with it." Reports from other Ivy universities were much the same.

"If there is a lesson in all this," the *Times* went on, "it is that a degree from a college like Harvard is no longer the guarantee of lifelong success that it used to be."

Decades ago in a static world, an Ivy degree was an asset in getting or keeping a job. By 2000, a Princeton graduate told me, the value of the Ivy diploma "lasts about fifteen minutes." In other words, it might open the door for the first job interview, but just about everyone changes jobs at least once in the first five years. After that, it is a person's own specific gravity that evaluates him. The name on the diploma has become irrelevant.

Furthermore, kids in college today, the demographers say, will be working at jobs or careers that don't yet exist. Thus, connections are no match for competence, which is the good small college's ace. For decades the good small colleges were outdoing the big and famous in a static world in producing America's scientists, scholars, and distinguished alumni listed in *Who's Who in America*. Now, in a fast-changing world, the field is tilted in their favor.

MYTH TWO: *If you can't make an Ivy, a prestige college is next best because the name on the diploma will determine whether you get into a good graduate school or have a good career.*

You can't get into any medical school or good graduate program with a C+ average from a name school, but you can with an even lower average from colleges such as New, Reed, Marlboro, and St. John's. Many others discussed in *Colleges That Change Lives* are tougher than any name school and have better medical and graduate school acceptance rates. Furthermore, the graduate admissions committee chairman and several committee members are likely as not to be alumni of small colleges. As for having a good career, the good small college will do more to empower you than any name school.

MYTH THREE: *Eastern institutions are the best and most desirable; southern schools are the least desirable; and forget about that dreary Siberian plain between Pennsylvania and the Colorado ski slopes known as the Midwest.*

Eastern cultural prejudice is responsible for this one. The truth is that some of the best, most innovative and life-changing colleges in the country are in the Midwest and South. Kalamazoo and Beloit pioneered in requiring foreign study and off-campus terms. One of their consortia, the Associated Colleges of the Midwest, started the Common Application way back in the 1960s, and it is now used by three hundred colleges, including Harvard. It pioneered an array of top-notch foreign and domestic study programs, self-designed programs, and a strong student voice in college governance.

Midwestern student bodies are more diversified than eastern ones. For example, no college has more diversity than Oberlin, which has admitted women, blacks, and Jews since the early 1830s. Grinnell and Beloit have about 29 percent Jews, which says two things about a college outside the East: high quality and diversity. Jews account for only 3 percent of the population, but yield to no group in their concern for good education, and so are less constrained by provincialism. There is no better college than Quaker Earlham, where a quarter of the students are children of college professors and administrators, a cogent point. Half the students come from more than five hundred miles away, and some years the freshman class has more Jews, Catholics, and Methodists than Quakers.

Similar things could be said about several colleges in the South. As a once hard-core integrationist, it was a struggle for me to decide to visit Millsaps because it is in Jackson, Mississippi. I now think there is no better college in the country, and nowhere do students have a keener sense of social responsibility. I also became a devout admirer of Hendrix in Arkansas and Austin and Southwestern in Texas. When black students in many northern campuses were segregating themselves, I found blacks sprinkled throughout the dining rooms of several southern colleges, and they told me the campuses were single communities socially.

MYTH FOUR: *A big university offers a broader, richer undergraduate experience with better teaching, wider course selection, and a more diversified student body than a college.*

This myth is so completely false that I had to write a separate chapter on it, "Why Small Is Best," to set things straight.

As pointed out in Myth One, the big university has forsaken liberal education. Ever since *Sputnik*, the big universities have become research institutes. All the rewards are for grantsmanship, publishing, and consulting. The chore of teaching is left to graduate assistants, or worse, to part-timers, most of whom can barely speak English. Thus, the claim that famous scholars improve the quality of teaching is a phony one that has misled people for years. The famous scholars are generally unhelpful, even hostile, to undergraduates. You will probably have to wait in line to get five minutes with one of them, if he actually does have office hours.

The big university may have two thousand courses, but they're all filled. If you do get in, it will probably be all lecture, and your grade will depend on one or two multiple-choice exams. In the small college the professor is your friend and mentor, and there is no limit to the breadth or depth of your collaborative explorations. Besides, after you've met the requirements for a major and the skeleton of a liberal education, there isn't much room left for the other 1,970 courses.

Even worse, budget crunches have made it so difficult to get the courses you need that it takes five and a half or six years to graduate in many popular public universities. That is why a flood of California refugees goes to college elsewhere.

Here is some firsthand testimony that points up the stark contrast:

Dr. Parker Marden, who went to Bates College and got his PhD from Brown, left the faculty at Cornell University (enrollment twenty thousand) to head a new sociology program at Lawrence University in Wisconsin (enrollment thirteen hundred). After a year he wrote, "I would contend that in a reasonable comparison of their faculties, the advantage rests with Lawrence, not with the major university I know best or others with which I am acquainted. At the very least, Lawrence fulfills its announced mission in undergraduate education while claiming little else, while the major universities meet many obligations while failing to meet the one about which they are most vocal: the teaching of undergraduates." The small size of the college community, Marden added, leads to greater visibility of the faculty and quick identification of incompetence, while at the big university anonymity hides inability.

Teaching at Lawrence, Marden said, is much harder, yet more persons do it well. For one thing, faculty have to be far more responsible for the student's education; they have close contact with the student and help him with his problems. At the big university, faculty hide from the students or refer them to graduate assistants. Faculty members are also more responsible for their disciplines; they have to teach students who have a broader, less career-oriented outlook and most of whom are majoring in other fields. Consequently,

Dr. Marden said, at Lawrence they have "a built-in crap detector."

"In my first term," he concluded, "I heard names that had been unmentioned in my presence since I left college: Plato, Swift, Emerson, Adam Smith, and others that I now recall to be rather central to a Western intellectual tradition."

MYTH FIVE: *A college you've heard about is better, or safer, than one you haven't.*

This is like buying a used car from a stranger. College presidents' knowledge of other institutions is not just limited, it's insular. Most of them are upwardly mobile executives with no sense of mission. As one of the good ones told me, "I never hear any discussion of educational matters at presidents' meetings." But they admire the entrepreneurial president and the basketball program that made George Mason University in Virginia a booming commuter institution. After its basketball publicity, applications soared, but the school was no better. An admissions director friend, griping about his president's mindset, said, "I read the *New York Times*. He reads the *Wall Street Journal*." At dinner a college president was telling me what a great job a friend was doing at Drew University and what a great school it was. I had been there a few weeks earlier and five faculty members had told me that about 5 percent of their students were interested in learning. I had found the library nearly empty on several visits, but the video games in the student center were doing an SRO business.

Guidance counselors don't get funds enough to enable them to case colleges on site, and as a result know little about them. And the institutions parents went to may not be the same places now.

As for magazine ratings of colleges, they are inherently phony. They measure input factors, many of which have nothing to do with empowering students. They know nothing about what happens during a student's four years or what the college produces. Years ago I was asked by *USA Today* to be one of their experts when it was considering competing with *US News and World Report*. I declined. I said such enterprises were a disservice to society, they were so misleading. There are few indicators of quality because there's never been any continuing and comparative product research. That's why myths such as this one fill the vacuum. Remember, a college does not get its name in the paper because it has a life-changing impact on a young mind and heart.

MYTH SIX: *What your friends say about a college is a good indicator.*

This is the feeblest reason of all. It shows that everyone doesn't like vanilla, and it exemplifies the adolescent need for peer approval. One year, 120 out of a Washington, D.C., suburban high school class of a little over 300 applied to Indiana University, one of many such pedestrian mass-production assembly lines. I don't know, but I'd bet that maybe half, or more, were mismatches who didn't graduate. Big state universities have attrition rates of up to 80 percent over four years.

Similarly, choosing a college to be with a boyfriend or girlfriend, or high school friends, is like believing in the tooth fairy. Why? Most college students change both love interests and majors at least once, but all teenagers are sure this high school love is a noble passion that will never end. One client and his girlfriend who'd been going together for four years planned to marry upon finishing at Macalaster. But eight weeks into their first semester, the boy's mother called me to say both had new loves.

Choosing a college to be with high school friends is just as foolish. Your and their paths have parted for good. Within a few weeks you will have a new set of friends. Guaranteed. Proven over a century of decades. You wouldn't keep in touch with them very long, anyway.

MYTH SEVEN: *You should make your college selection early in your senior year and have all your applications in by Christmas or thereabouts.*

More than any other bit of brainwashing to which the public is subjected about education, this manifestation of the Chicken Little syndrome has made a scramble out of what should be an unhurried and painstaking process of investigation, self-examination, and deliberate, informed decision.

The sky does not fall in January, February, or March. In the academic community, only about eighty colleges, mostly eastern, can enforce winter application deadlines. These have uniform early decision, and mid-April reply dates. But they take only seventy thousand or so—about 3 percent of the top students—out of the 2.5 million freshmen applicants. Most colleges use rolling admissions—acting on applications as they come in—or their deadlines don't mean much because they don't have the luxury of having two or more applicants for every bed. Never once, even during the Vietnam draft, have all the colleges been full.

Of course, if you're one of the thirteen thousand or so going to one of the Ivies, Little Ivies, or what used to be the Seven Sisters, you'd better be prompt about getting in your applications. And if you're one of the fifty thousand odd headed for one of the other early-deadline, very selective colleges, this is also true.

But since the only law that governs admissions is supply and demand, most of the good small colleges that can't be that selective are taking students well into the summer, depending on the flow of applications. If the admissions staff hasn't filled its class by spring, they're getting pretty nervous and will often accept applicants they would have turned down the previous fall or winter.

MYTH EIGHT: *The most selective college is the most challenging.*

Nonsense. This is a favorite parental code word for selectivity, and it has nothing to do with major or challenge. Before the GI Bill swamped higher education's capacity, the A, B, and C students and the ne'er-do-wells all went to college together and sat in the same classes. Furthermore, the education was better then because a mix of abilities is crucial: the middle group asks the questions that the bright ones are ashamed or afraid to ask, and that the bottom group doesn't think of. Three of the most intellectual colleges, St. John's, Marlboro, and New, are not selective. The fourth, Reed, wasn't until things were changed by the growth of college-going and by this book and its companion, *Colleges That Change Lives*.

MYTH NINE: *The college catalog will inform you whether or not this school is for you.*

Not likely. Read enough of them, and they become a blur, because if there's one characteristic they share, it's interchangeability. Diversity, along with availability, is one of the boasts of American higher education—what with 2,000 four-year and 1,000 two-year institutions. One might expect, therefore, as a professor observed twenty years ago, that browsing through a collection of catalogs would give a heady hint of variety, of intellectual adventures offered by all this educational imagination, and solid answers on how each of these institutions sees its role and purpose and how it differs from the others in developing personal intellect and character.

What one discovers is that with a few notable exceptions, catalogs all say the same thing. Education is a status-conscious, follow-the-leader industry in which obvious tub-thumping is bad form, but in which there is always intense competition for students. The catalog and the view book are the chief sales pitches, with the former camouflaged as an internal document. What the public relations department or a dean may write in the section on philosophy may or may not be read by the faculty members or teaching assistants who confront the students in the classrooms. Indeed, some catalogs and view books are farmed-out jobs, glossily packaged by commercial firms who provide the prose content as well as the slick cover.

Things haven't changed for the better in the half century since the late Harry Gideonse, president of Brooklyn College, said that if the Federal Trade Commission ever started prosecuting colleges for false and misleading advertising, there'd be more college than corporation presidents under cease and desist orders.

MYTH TEN: *Your college should be bigger than your high school.*

It should be smaller if you're in a large suburban high school. See the chapter "Why Small Is Best." Teenagers often think five or ten thousand bodies will provide a smorgasbord of attractive, attentive members of the opposite sex and lots of activity, especially if high school has been a painful ugly-duckling stage or if they've gone to tiny single-sex schools.

The answer lies not in the number, but the kind of people. Every good college is striving for all the diversity it can get: in race, creed, and social and economic background and in interests and personal qualities. Public institutions, on the other hand, except for Michigan and Virginia, admit by formula based on grades, class rank, and test scores. Out-of-state admittees are limited, and the bulk of the in-staters may be several notches lower in ability and attractiveness. Also, it is easier to know everyone in a small group or city than in a big one. As a client said after a year at the University of Maryland, "I miss the diversity we had at Walt Whitman," her high school. In other words, six hundred available males is better than six thousand unavailable males, especially if the mix is better.

As for activities, in the small college everybody can participate; everyone is a walk-on. In the big school only the stars or the specialists get an opportunity, whether in sports, dramatics, publications, or what have you.

Most of the good small colleges are not in cities, and if they didn't have lots of good activities and special attractions, they'd be ghost campuses. The truth is that there are usually more things to do on any good campus than any one person could take advantage of.

MYTH ELEVEN: *Going more than two hundred miles away from home means a costlier education and probable isolation.*

It may be cheaper to go six hundred, eight hundred, or a thousand miles away if doing so improves the campus job opportunities or helps get financial aid. Indeed, as discussed in chapter 16, with some aid packages it can be cheaper to go far away to an expensive college than to live at home and go to a low-cost or even free public institution. Furthermore, travel costs on low-cost carriers may not be nearly as great as parents fear. If the student is in a good school, trips home will be few even the freshman year, because the library should demand some weekend time. After the freshman year, they may be only two a year. And availability of an airport is often more relevant than the distance in miles from home.

MYTH TWELVE: *If you're in the top 10 percent of your class in a good, big high school and have SATs of 1300 or better,*

you belong in an Ivy or Little Ivy to get the kind of education you should have.

That notion is ridiculous. You will get a better education at any one of scores of good small colleges than at any Ivy. And you'll have to work harder, a lot harder.

MYTH THIRTEEN: *Ivy League schools are looking for students who don't have excellent grades.*

This hardy perennial is a misreading of something that every intelligent admissions officer has always tried to do: attract people who have done something. It is often grasped at by parents of underachievers who may have heard of a much-publicized foundation grant to Williams College in the 1950s to finance an admissions-risk program for boys who had achieved outside of school. To be accurate, the myth should read: Good colleges are looking for students who have something to offer *besides* good grades and scores. If that something is impressive enough, the grades may not have to be excellent, but they can't be bad.

One of my young friends with an SAT total of just over 820 on the old 1600 scale, and a C+ average, was accepted by Amherst, but after high school he had won a Bronze Star in Vietnam and was doing a good job managing a bar. Another with a strong B average excited every admissions director I talked to because he had taught himself calculus in two summers and then took a semester of it and got a B to prove he knew it. He taught himself to play the piano and played

Rachmaninoff; sold more tickets to the Boy Scout fair than anyone in the county; and was an authority on Appalachian butterflies, discovering a species new to Maryland and writing a monograph on it.

Years ago, before Princeton was quite so tough to get into, the undergraduate dean came to me one spring day with what he rightly thought was a good Sunday story for the *New York Times*. He and his fellow administrators had been disturbed to discover, in going over the dossiers of the senior class, that many of the men who seemed most likely to reflect credit on Princeton were persons of accomplishment who otherwise had been marginal admittees, some with SAT scores in the low 400s.

MYTH FOURTEEN: *SAT scores are the most important thing. Good ones will get you in, and poor ones will keep you out.*

Wrong. Many colleges don't even require them. First comes excellent grades in the toughest program available, then comes rank in class if it's a big suburban high school. Rank isn't nearly as important in a class of fifty, in a good school. Then comes what you say about yourself in your application, then SAT scores and what you've done. In other words, the whole picture. Some Ivies, however, particularly Dartmouth, do put considerable reliance on SATs in making their decisions.

MYTH FIFTEEN: *A coaching course will improve your SAT scores and hence your chances.*

No prep course is going to lift a 400-bracket verbal scorer into the 600 level. No matter what else the disputants say in this hotly argued issue, this just won't happen—ruling out some freak occurrence—because the verbal part is a test of the range of a person's vocabulary, how well he can analyze a paragraph and write. Naturally, no quick fix can do the work of a long habit of reading good books. A seventeen-year-old who has had little interest and little practice in these skills for eleven school years isn't likely to become adept in a few weeks.

The verbal score and the amount and kind of reading a person has done are like ski tracks. I've never known a non-reader to have a high verbal score, nor a good reader to have a low one.

What is "good" reading? It's not just anything between book covers. Too many teenagers share the mistaken belief of a young friend who had a verbal score of 45 on the PSAT, but who insisted that he "read a lot." "What kind of things?" I asked. "Fantasy, action, *Harry Potter*, things like that." I handed him a compilation of the kinds of books read by kids who'd gone to Mount Holyoke over the last few decades. He studied it for a minute or two and with a look of incredulity asked, "These are books kids actually read in their spare time?"

If a prep course is long enough and requires enough homework, it usually helps the very low scorers—if they really work at it—to improve their vocabularies and reading and test-taking skills. Since the test is of "developed ability," as the Educational Testing Service (ETS) says, the longer and more demanding the course, the more it's likely to help. Youths with a reading habit aren't as likely to be helped much, since they already have the tools and tend to score in the 600s or better anyway. And I've known of some clients whose scores have dropped after a prep course. A prep course is much more likely to boost the math score, and ETS has long said it is helpful to be taking a good math course at the time.

If, after a prep course, one's scores go up 30 or 40 points each in the verbal and math, nothing has really been accomplished, for normal growth will account for that much annual improvement. Rarely have I known of 100-point increases in the verbal score, and they were unusual cases. In one, a boy worked hard for ten weeks and raised his score into the 400s. Another, who had had a learning difficulty, was drilled for several weeks on the Latin roots of words and brought his verbal into the 500s. And now there is a writing section.

But if your scores take a big jump, say from 1000 to 1400 on the verbal and math, from one year to the next, a good admissions officer will toss out the higher scores; they're out of the pattern.

MYTH SIXTEEN: *A bad recommendation from a teacher or counselor will ruin your chances of getting into a good college.*

It cannot if what the teacher or counselor says is not true, and sometimes even if it is true. So parents, don't be afraid: criticize the bad teacher; take a stand against the injustice or the stupidity. Too often a bad school problem goes uncorrected because parents fear that complaining will imperil their child.

One negative opinion running counter to the general estimate of a student won't hurt him any more than one bad grade, probably less. The admissions director is going to look at the whole picture. If there is a teacher conflict and a bad grade, or the prospect of a bad recommendation, deal with it honestly, putting all the cards on the table in the application. That will do two things: impress the admissions director because there's nothing so refreshing and winning as candor, and help take the steam, if any, out of the negative comment, particularly if it is unwarranted.

Remember, admissions directors are sensible people aware of failings in teachers as well as in students, and they don't believe everything they read. As one of the Little Ivy admissions directors said, "I always apply the filter factor."

MYTH SEVENTEEN: *Your choice of major will decide your career path. Therefore, the quality of that department should govern your choice of college.*

This mistake has led many people into the wrong choices. One of the most overrated things about college is the imagined importance of the major. There's only one chance in ten that a person will be doing anything connected with his college major ten or fifteen years out of college. That's what every survey of alumni finds. Furthermore, since most eighteen-year-olds know very little about themselves or the world, and nothing about what variety of choices may be open to them a decade ahead, the versatile preparation of a liberal education is the most practical course, and early specialization the least.

Indeed, an early choice of major ought to be resisted or avoided so as to spend a couple of years sampling around and getting a broad groundwork. Most students change direction at least once, often twice. Besides, no matter what the major, four years of college won't produce a practitioner in any field that isn't mere formula and routine. Medical schools care only about the biology, chemistry, physics, and science major. There's no such thing as a prelaw major; no first-rate college has an undergraduate journalism major; and if you want to be an anthropologist or archaeologist, the graduate school would prefer a history major.

In engineering, the area that demands the earliest full commitment, the attrition rate is highest. Nationally, about 30 percent finish the course.

The choice of college should be governed by what the ethos and the intellectual force of that place seem likely to do for you as a person.

MYTH EIGHTEEN: *A high school diploma is needed to get into college.*

Heavens, no. I've had a few clients go on to college at the end of their sophomore years, and a lot at the end of their junior years. The sophomores have been very bright and voracious learners. Juniors have no problem if their records are good, they're socially mature enough, and another year in high school would be a bore or a waste. Good colleges have been doing this for a long time, but they do it on an individual, case-by-case basis.

For the nineteen-year-old and older, the General Educational Development (GED) Test will do quite nicely, even if you have never set foot in a high school. Years ago, a twenty-two-year-old who had dropped out in the ninth grade not only got into and did well in college, but also reached the final cut for a major graduate award. And GED alumni do well in college; they're motivated.

MYTH NINETEEN: *Going to a private prep school will enhance your chances of getting into a good college.*

Quite often the opposite is true. While a few of the most prestigious prep schools may have Ivy graduates as college counselors as well as doing a nonpareil job in the classroom to give their kids an edge, a high rank in a big, competitive suburban high school is usually a lot more persuasive to any admissions officer than high rank in a small private school. A Little Ivy admissions director once said, "Walt Whitman [in Bethesda, Maryland] is the best high school in the United States; at least I get more students from there."

The highly competitive private school can be a liability if a good student winds up with a much lower class rank than he would have had in his public school. The private schools are of such variable quality that the college admissions director wants to know whether it's tough or easy. If a transfer from a public school is getting markedly better grades at the private one, it will look like a trade of high tuition for high grades.

MYTH TWENTY: *Millions of dollars in unused scholarships are going begging every year.*

This pie-in-the-sky phony has been fooling folks every year for half a century. I get scores and scores of hopeful calls every year. It benefits only the scam artists and the peddlers of books on the subject. With the cost of college soaring, it has spawned a cottage industry of so-called financial aid advisers and others who promise to "find" so many sources of aid. The advisers may help fill out the financial aid form as adroitly as possible or help shuffle assets around so the student appears eligible for aid.

Of the many financial aid directors I have asked over the years, not one has ever known of a case where anyone got more than $500 of this treasure. As one said, "If it's not being used, it's because it can't be used." In other words, the criteria for eligibility are weird.

You can get a database at your high school that lists all scholarships available nationally as well as in your area.

The truth is that there never has been more than a fraction of the money needed and applied for every year. At least 95 percent of all aid is channeled through the colleges. Unless you have veteran's benefits or one of your parents works for a firm with a scholarship program, the chance of finding such money outside the college channels is pretty slim to none. The various garden clubs, Legion posts, and so on that do give "scholarships" do so in pittances that would barely pay for a semester's textbooks. As chapter 16 will tell you, the financial aid office of the college that accepts you is the best place to go for help. That's what those folks want to do, free.

MYTH TWENTY-ONE: *A good college is hard to get into.*

Even at the crest of the college-going boom in the 1950s or in the 1970 panic to avoid the Vietnam War, this was a myth. Anyone—whether an average or poor student, or a problem learner—can have a choice of places that will help him grow. And after 2009, when the teenage population begins shrinking, there'll be even more choices. That's what this book is all about.

CHAPTER 2

Looking Beyond the Ivy League: Where the Buyer's Market Is

IF WHAT YOU WANT is a good education instead of status, your college search will be worry-free and fruitful. Even with the college-going army peaking in 2009, you can have several choices, and they'll do more for you and your future than the status schools.

Two events since this book first came out would have seismic effects if it weren't for cultural lag. The public takes many years to fully appreciate something new and different. But both events are destined at least to lessen the feverish herd struggle to get into the designer-label schools, the Ivies and their clones.

First came the corporate downsizing upheaval of the early 1990s detailed in the "Twenty-one Myths" chapter, which proved once and for all that the name on the diploma is meaningless when corporate layoffs come. It once was true that the name on the diploma governed promotions as well as hiring, but no more. Now competence, not connections, makes the difference.

The second event was the exposé, also described in chapter 1, "Twenty-one Myths," that liberal education in the research universities is "a project in ruins." But liberal education is alive and well in the good small colleges, and that's where the buyer's market is.

The central message of this book is that there is a lot of high-quality education (which Ivy types lack) available, and it's available for many different kinds of students, not just those sweating for the Ivies.

The Department of Education says that while the number of high school graduates is peaking at 3,264,000 in 2009, it is anybody's guess how that will affect the market. In many of the most populous states, up to half the increase (from 2,900,000 in 2000) will be Asians, Hispanics, and African-Americans.

It is important to remember that selectivity is no measure of the good college—either how challenging it is, what it will do for you, or how hard you'll have to work. Hiram tops the Ivies on all three counts, and it usually takes 85 percent of all who apply. The Ivies skim off 10 to 20 percent of the A students. Just to emphasize that point, three of the four most intellectual colleges, Marlboro, New, and St. John's, aren't selective. The fourth, Reed, which once accepted up to 95 percent, has become selective since *Colleges That Change Lives* came out. Eva Brann, former St. John's dean, said, "We're about as selective as a pickup baseball team." Of course, kids don't apply to those four unless they're willing to pay the price.

It should also be underscored that many of the colleges that produce the highest percentages of future PhDs and alumni in *Who's Who* accept 70 to 90 percent of all who apply.

Faculty members at small colleges who have also taught at elite institutions, when asked if they noticed any difference in the two groups of students, invariably say something like, "All the difference in the world. At the elite schools they were learning for the sake of grades; here they're learning for the sake of learning." The inference is easy: the community where learning is valued for its own sake is much more likely to affect the development of values and the ability and desire to go on learning and to grow than is the community where learning is a means, not an end.

The message that there are many little-known keys to the good life is similar to Thomas Gray's observation that "Full many a gem of purest ray serene, / The dark unfathomed caves of ocean bear." But it is a message that is faintly heard for many reasons. Among them are the college-going boom, the failings of counseling, the lack of consumer research on colleges, indolent consumerism, and the designer-label college syndrome.

Education was destined to become a twentieth-century growth industry. The country's enormous economic and population growth, its vast wealth and commitment to education for all, and the vast growth of knowledge in every field all helped to ensure that. Only about 10 percent of the teenage population went to college just before World War II. Then the GI Bill opened the door to the hundreds of thousands of returning veterans. By the end of the Korean War the boom was on, nearly swamping the colleges. The percentage hit 50 on its way to 60, and higher education became a seller's market, such as that the automobile dealers had after World War II when Detroit's assembly lines worked around the clock to satisfy the national hunger for cars instead of tanks.

From then on, college became a consuming family anxiety. In 1958, at the height of the tension, an official of the College Entrance Examination Board, who had spoken the night before to a packed house of parents at a New Jersey suburban high school, was asked if there was much concern about his subject, the SATs. He replied, "If you could have plugged in that audience, you'd have lit up the whole town." Today, he would have enlarged on that.

The boom was driven by the certain knowledge that a bachelor's degree was a union card, the requirement for first-class citizenship in the American economic establishment. Just going to college wasn't sufficient; one had to stay the course or else. And those who didn't believe it were soon enough, and usually painfully enough, made converts. There are countless variations on the story of my friend Bobby. Because he didn't take his comprehensive exams at Sewanee, he didn't get his degree, but he was nevertheless unconcerned. With four years of college on his record, he was confident he would zoom right to the top in his chosen field, the construction industry. After months of toil he was still a laborer with no prospects, so a friend got him a job in a major insurance company, which surely would be more appreciative. Again, the story was the same: no degree, no place on the ladder. So he quit his job and with considerable pain and toil went back and got his degree. All of a sudden he was on the ladder, climbing, and twenty years later was in the company's upper-middle management. And in the early 1990s he was not downsized, but many Ivy alums were.

The boom years have created a supplicant rather than a hard-nosed consumer mentality in parents, students, and counselors. College catalogs say, "Applications should be made early in the fall of the senior year," and high school counselors help by pressuring students to get their applications in early, when for most colleges this is not only unnecessary but may penalize a student.

Why? Because it is essential that the young buyer examine and test the merchandise, by making visits to the colleges. In October, November, and December, applications may be coming in at a rate that augurs two applicants for every bed, which may induce delusions of selectivity and result in the rejection of some early applicants. But in February, the flow may be a trickle, and most of those accepted usually choose other colleges. It's a fortunate college that gets a 50 percent yield. Thus the admissions director, faced with the prospect of empty beds and qualms about his job, may find applicants that he would have turned down in November very attractive. As one of the veterans in the business said at lunch one April day, "I'd be happy to see some of those people I turned down last fall come through my door now."

Admissions directors, incidentally, are the most nomadic group in our society, more so even than football coaches. Both groups live and die by the numbers. Every private college has financial worries, and if the sales office isn't filling the beds, it becomes the scapegoat. (Nearly every new college president thinks a new admissions director is going to bring in hordes of new students. It seldom works that way, however.) Of course a college would love to have its freshman class filled and guaranteed by Thanksgiving or Christmas, but many of them won't fill up until late summer, if at all.

Variations in quality, ambience, and ethos can be seen only by asking pointed and embarrassing questions of administrators, students, and faculty members in visits to at least two or three colleges. This takes time. Some of it should be done in the junior year, but because kids change so much so fast, it is important that they do some more comparison shopping in their senior year.

With counselors pressing for hasty decisions, too little of this is done. Inevitably, the situation produces anguish. Every winter I get anxious calls from parents whose children have applied to the wrong colleges and fear the game is up because a counselor has said it is too late; counselors should know better.

Once in a while a counselor has told a youngster that she is not college material. That should be forbidden; it's cruel and almost never true. Every high school should have a sign prominently displayed that reads, "If you can make it here, you can make it in a college." The truth is that anyone who graduates from any kind of a decent high school in a college prep program, and a lot who don't, can get into many colleges and can have a good college experience. They may have to take summer school courses or go to a junior college first, but one way or another, the door is open to just about everyone who's willing to make the effort. I've seen students with verbal scores in the low 300s on the old 1600 scale, bad high school records, and many with learning problems make it through college. I've had clients with verbal scores in the 400s (old scale) graduate with honors from Duke and Vassar, among others. One girl with a 500 verbal made Phi Beta Kappa. Amherst accepted one client of mine with a 412 verbal, and I know of another who had a 317 (both old scale).

After I'd vented my gripes one day about admissions directors' heavy reliance on SAT scores to the late Eugene S. (Bill) Wilson, Amherst admissions dean, he said, "Several years ago in our freshman football game with Williams we had a tackle who spent the afternoon in the Williams backfield. A Williams admissions officer nudged a faculty member next to him and said, 'See that boy; he won't be back next year, he only had a three-seventeen verbal.' But he was, and in the next three years spent three more afternoons in the Williams backfield and graduated. I knew he could do it because he and another boy in the same high school had identical records in the same heavy schedule, and the other boy had a verbal score in the six hundreds."

Also, doors once closed to the underachiever are now open, as they are to the sinner and, fortunately, to the student with a learning problem. In the 1970s and early 1980s, programs to help students with learning disabilities and problems mushroomed, and often it is harder to get a place in one of those new programs than to get into the college itself, so popular have they become. It only took the public discovery of the word *dyslexia* to reveal all manner of related problems in need of help. In many colleges, help without formal programs is given by caring faculty members who may not be specialists but who are effective teachers. A student who has dyslexic problems may not only get a good deal of one-on-one tutoring, but he may also be permitted to take his exams orally and to tape-record papers.

Large universities have aid available in learning centers or even formal programs. But the instructor in the classroom may not be part of or even sympathetic to the effort, as one of my young friends learned to her sorrow. Convinced she'd have more social life if she went to Tulane, she chose that school over one of the good small colleges we discussed. She had a 3.2 average in a competitive high school, despite her learning disability, but at the university she got no help from the learning center or the professors and couldn't make her grades. And she had to spend so much time studying that she had no social life. Her father said the learning center's director saw her job as educating the faculty. At a good small college, the girl's teachers would have given her extra time for exams or otherwise helped her along. Their concern is for the undergraduate, their only reason for being. It is not only a matter of mission but also of the profit motive—a job.

And when there is such collaboration, the student is much more likely to be able to conquer his problems. I have had young friends with a wide spectrum of handicaps make it through college, and with steadily increasing ability. One, whose dyslexia wasn't discovered until he was in the eleventh grade in a New England prep school, got help and worked at his problem and has long since graduated from Ohio Wesleyan. Another who was certified as legally blind in high school and who did a lot of work with tapes made an impressive enough record at Hiram College to get a graduate fellowship at Carnegie-Mellon. And they are just two of dozens with just about every conceivable kind of learning disability who have done well in college and have been done well by the college.

The underachiever, whose options were often limited to junior colleges in the 1960s, now can get into colleges that wouldn't have looked at him in the past. And if the under-achiever or the sinner has good test scores, his range of choices is broader now.

Late spring or summer applications are often a must for the marginal applicant or someone with a learning problem, simply because the college wants as much recent informa-tion as it can get. The marginal applicant is usually the un-derachiever. I had cases every year where an admissions director would say, "Let's wait and see how he does when all the returns are in this June and then call me." And unless the client stopped working, he usually got in. This sort of thing happens at colleges of varying degrees of rigor. A C– student may be on his mettle to make Cs and Bs, or a B+ student to improve on a D or a C grade from the previous term. The point is that many colleges are eager to open the door way past Christmas.

The winter deadlines are mainly for those who have straight-A or nearly straight-A records, high SAT scores, sev-eral advanced placement or honors courses, and programs that show four years each of math, science, language, and English, as well as substantial out-of-class achievements.

The phrase "substantial out-of-class achievements" is crucial. Parents too often say, "With her grades and test scores she can get in anywhere." Absolutely and positively not so. Many an applicant with straight As and 1500 on the SATs and nothing else has been rejected by colleges a lot less selective than Harvard or Princeton, for that kind of record indicates a grind, which means an undesirable. The admissions director at Carleton reacted to one such of my clients with, "That kind goes on the heap pretty fast." Carleton takes about 40 to 45 percent of its applicants—all of whom are excellent students—compared with 11 or 12 percent by Harvard or Princeton. On the other hand, Carleton often has more National Merit Scholars than any four-year college in the country.

For the vast majority there is a lot more time to shop. And if they take the trouble to investigate some of the colleges with rolling admissions like Eckerd, for example, they will encounter stimuli that will do more for them in the long run than a Cornell or a Penn.

The shopping should be done with the right attitude— not "Am I good enough for the college?" but rather "Is it good enough for me?" But first, in order to decide, the student has to confront himself with some basic questions, such as Why am I going? and What do I want of this experience? The consumer approach is the only sensible one, not simply because college is expensive, but because the experience can develop a person's ability to think critically and imaginatively, to make informed, intelligent connections, and to develop a value system that will affect the kind of person she becomes. It will also give her the prepared brain that can visualize and seize new opportunities. Serendipity.

The undergraduate college's superior potency has been demonstrated by a good deal of comparison of institutional productivity in recent decades. Tabulations of the baccalaureate origins of people who had achieved listings in *Who's Who* done in the late 1950s and forty years later in 1989 both show the entries crowded with graduates of little-known and not very selective colleges.

The good small college will also be seen as the fertile seedbed for the nation's thinkers as well as doers. Congress, as well as most laymen, always assumed that the famous big universities were the source of the nation's scientific and intellectual strength. Consequently, these institutions got most of the federal funds for science education and research. But in the mid-1980s, and again at the turn of the century, digging into performance records revealed that the good small colleges are giving the nation the most brains for the bucks. The figures hardly change at all.

News stories of Harvard's three hundred and fiftieth anniversary made much of the line, "Its faculty has produced 27 Nobel laureates." Not so. Twenty-four graduated from other colleges, 7 from City College of New York. In the eighty-four Nobel years up to that point, the most sought after college in the land produced only 9, and all of the Ivies only 27 of the 137 American laureates. The Little Ivies—Amherst, Wesleyan, and Williams—struck out (but the next year, as I was informed by a terse note from the assistant to the president, Amherst finally scored with 1). Little Swarthmore had produced 6; Oberlin, 3; and Wooster, 2.

The popular conception may be that the Washington establishment is peopled chiefly with Ivy Leaguers, but the reality is different. Reed, with about eleven hundred students, has over 150 alumni in prestigious and intellectually demanding Washington jobs. The immediate reaction to this—that this is due to old-boy networks—may be true. But

the fact that there are so many Reed alumni in these posi-
tion also means that faculty members take an interest in
individual students, that the students perform on the job,
and that they in turn have confidence in their schools' products and therefore can afford to continue populating the
network.

The good small colleges are even better door-openers to
graduate and professional schools. The graduate department
chairman who reads the applications often has gone to one
of these small schools. He knows that in the university the
undergraduate is a second-class citizen who gets cheated with
big classes, much graduate-assistant teaching, and faculty
whose interest is in research and publishing and working
with PhD candidates because that's where the pay and prestige—and job tenure—are. He knows that the small-college
faculty member who recommends a student has worked
closely with him, whereas in a university the professors may
barely know the student. And he knows that students from
these colleges have done well not only as graduate students,
but also in their careers.

Acceptance records to medical and graduate school support this. In some recent years, for example, Wooster has had
a 100 percent medical school acceptance rate, compared
with a 33 percent rate for all colleges. The University of
Wisconsin medical school will accept Beloit juniors. At
Knox, seniors can do their final college year and their first
year at Rush Medical College simultaneously, in Knox classrooms. Many colleges that aren't very selective have medical
school acceptance rates over 85 percent, so it boils down to
a matter of the applicant's own performance. A good record

at any one of scores of good small colleges is better than a lesser one at Harvard.

If these unknown schools are so good, why aren't they deluged with applicants? There are several reasons, any one of which may be enough to turn up a teenager's nose. First off, most people are provincial; to easterners, a college not in the Northeast—unless it's in California, Colorado, or Florida—is suspect, and so is the region. And almost anywhere, a high school senior may be challenged by peers and counselors for wanting an out-of-state college. Anti-South prejudice is less now than it was in the 1960s and 1970s, but the Midwest still suffers from some vague image of its being a vast prairie inhabited by hayseeds who've never been out of their counties.

Another is the eastern mystique: if it's in the East, it's not only better, but its student body is more sophisticated. To students living on the East Coast, it may be closer to home, and the teenager has probably heard of it. Indeed, to the millions along the Atlantic seaboard, anything in the East is closer than anything west of the Appalachians; a father once questioned my credibility for telling him that Cleveland was closer to Washington than Boston. So many clients have objected to exiling a child to the Chicago or St. Louis area but have found New Orleans, Miami, or Portland, Maine, comfortably close that it gives rise to Pope's Law of Geographic Distances: Any distance west from Washington is twice the same distance north or south.

And remember the myth that anyone with a grain of sense knows—a school you've heard of has to be better and safer than one you haven't. There's also the adolescent embarrassment that one's friends have never heard of a school. When a college gets its name in the papers, parents start asking about it.

The sheep instinct is responsible for the "hot college" syndrome that lets the bargains go unnoticed. Like teenage dress fashions, its rationale is that the college is acceptable because one's peers approve, or are talking about it. The sheep instinct is a status affliction that short-circuits thinking and alters perceptions. This disease is often transmitted from this year's college freshmen back to their high schools' seniors and juniors and thence to parents. It makes a school that no one may have heard of five years ago seem very desirable all of a sudden and a key to the good life, however pedestrian that school remains academically. Worse, this affliction obscures the variety of good choices that are available, even to the below-average student in a buyer's market.

Finally, there is the Groucho Marx "I wouldn't belong to any club that would have me as a member" syndrome. In the worried 1960s, a young client, who I'm sure had never heard of Groucho's crack, blurted out when I told him Knox College would accept him, "It can't be any good if it would take me." (There is no better college in the country.) While his outburst was unique, his reaction was a fairly common one. After having been brainwashed for two decades by a seller's market into believing that any reputable college plays hard to get, many people continue to find the idea of easy acceptance suspect. And for a teenager with a fragile self-image because she is not in the top rank of a competitive high school class and so can't hope for one of the popular schools, it is especially difficult to believe.

The average student will have more and more good choices if she will only open her eyes and her mind and look, unafraid of her peers' opinions. But as one exasperated mother said, "All these kids want is designer-label colleges."

And that's too bad.

CHAPTER 3

Why Small Is Best

IT IS NONSENSE TO THINK that bigger is better, especially in education. The good small liberal arts college will give you the best and most challenging education. It also will make you a better person, a more independent and creative thinker than the university. The small college produces the pioneers and risk takers who will prosper in the new world. At the small college you will make long-lasting friendships with your professors. The university fails on all these counts. In fact, such things are not on its agenda; it thinks it has bigger fish to fry. (Japanese universities, however, forced to compete for students due to a falling birth rate, are copying the forty small schools in *Colleges That Change Lives*.)

After *Sputnik*, federal dollars for research to catch up with the Russians changed the universities into research institutes. By now, as detailed in chapter 1, their commitment to Mammon is so binding that a noted Princeton scholar, Stanley N. Katz, president emeritus of the American Council of Learned Societies, has warned that liberal education in them "is a project in ruins" that threatens "the vitality" of American democracy. They're "uncomfortable with values," and values are central to the good small college. His indictment includes not only the Ivies and their clones but scores of wannabees.

Nevertheless, Dr. Katz says, "liberal education is alive and well in the small colleges." "Small" comes in many sizes, from Marlboro's 300 to St. Olaf's or Hope's 3,200. But student bodies much larger than that dilute the sense of community.

There is no magic curriculum, program, or method, for the good small colleges do many different things. The magic lies in how they do it. Students and professors collaborate rather than compete. Discussion of values is emphasized. Students are heavily involved in their own education; they work with each other and with their teachers. It is collaborative, not competitive. They coauthor research papers or books with their teachers and so are a big step ahead in graduate school and in many jobs. They are hiking or dinner companions or intramural teammates, and in these relaxed occasions get insights from bright minds across the spectrum of scholarship. This is cross-fertilization and making connections. It is part of the students' search to find themselves, and may be as or more important than what happens in the classroom. It is just what the adolescent mind needs at this stage. If a student feels the need, he can specialize later, and more profitably, when he's more mature. He may come to college expecting a career in biology or international relations and wind up as a music or physics major. This is the kind of intellectual stimulus the small college offers, as Dr. Sam Shulman points out in his book *Old Main*, an examination of a dozen small colleges.

A vital ingredient that makes for far better teachers is that the good small college changes professors' lives, too. At college after college across the country, faculty members would give me variations of what a professor at Hendrix said: "I came here expecting to stay a few years and move on to a research university, but now you couldn't blast me out of here." They also would say that nowhere else had they experienced such collegiality, lack of politics and infighting, or freedom to disagree and remain friends. Or, as a professor who'd had tenure at Vanderbilt said, "My smallest class there was seventy-five. I wanted to be with students and talk with them." Such avowals reflect the secret ingredient that helps work the magic of the good small college that the university turns its nose up at.

The university offers a different kind of depth in one field and on the graduate level. It is an aggregate of scholars whose focus is on research to increase knowledge and on graduate students. Undergraduates are nuisances that subsidize research and get short shrift. They may never have a conversation with a professor, or even write a paper.

The intellectual awakening in the small college is passionately voiced for uncounted thousands in other schools in the words of a Hiram junior: "Many catalytic things have happened to me. These are incredible people. They love to teach. We have a mentor relationship. They are always making cross-connections from one area or discipline to another. They are always encouraging, pushing me to do better. There is so much pressure, so many responsibilities it forces you to keep going. They say 'this might be a publishable paper.' One would like to come back here to teach—or to one like it."

Her testimonial reminded me of a Hiram freshman and client, years earlier, who'd written his mother: "I've never had to work so hard in all my life! This place is great!" Both of these comments are echoed in the Ten Years Later sections at the end of the college profiles in the second edition of *Colleges That Change Lives*, as well as in comments I've received from clients over a period of nearly forty years. In fact, one girl wrote on the cover of her graduation invitation: "Loren, Kalamazoo really did change my life!"

But from clients who've gone to an Ivy or Ivy clone (often against my advice), I've never heard such a testimonial. One client told me on a visit there, "It's hard to be humble at Amherst." A mother called to report her disappointed daughter had written, "Michigan is everything Mr. Pope said it was and I'm going to transfer." A junior in Michigan's honors program, like many at other universities, couldn't get a single needed class in her major. As a girl who came to me after a year at the University of Florida said, "They may have two thousand courses, but try to get in one; you're bound to get screwed."

And a dentist friend and his wife persuaded their son to transfer from Washington University in St. Louis, a first-rate school, to the University of Wisconsin because it was bigger and had more facilities, and therefore would be a better entrée into medical school. They were wrong. Wisconsin rejected him, but the medical school admission director at Washington U. told me they would have taken him because he was a known commodity, and the profs who gave him recommendations were known to the medical school admissions committee. He finally got the last-gasp acceptance at another medical school.

Many a parent has written to say they wish they'd had as good experiences as their kids who'd gone to good small colleges. One father told me, "I didn't know what a lousy experience I'd had at the University of Texas until I read your books." A Duke professor, who'd written an article saying "learning is optional" there, told me at the time, "You don't have to do any work to get a B here, and I think the same thing is true at other elite schools." His daughter went to a good small college.

During my counseling career, faculty members from Harvard, MIT, Johns Hopkins, Michigan, Wisconsin, Georgetown, George Washington, American, Maryland, West Virginia, Duke, North Carolina, and others I don't recall brought their children to me, expecting them to go to a small college.

And finally, the small colleges have been outperforming the big ones in producing America's future scientists, scholars, and other contributors ever since record-keeping began in 1920.

CHAPTER 4

Is the Teaching Better in the Good Small College?

SMALL COLLEGE STUDENTS SAY NOTHING can match their profs. Those in the book *Colleges That Change Lives* believe theirs are the smartest people in the world, terrific teachers and wonderful friends. Those forty schools are catalytic liberal arts colleges, but they're not selective.

A Harvard Graduate School of Education survey of 4,500 young professors in 2006 showed why they say their teachers are world-beaters. The young tenure-track faculty said respect, collegiality, and department climate were more important than salary—five times more important, in fact. This was a marked shift from previous generations. For the older professors, autonomy in the workplace—including protection for their political opinions—was the main concern. The present generation is much more concerned with quality of life in the department; they like working in teams and want senior faculty members to take an interest in their work, collaborate with them, and treat them fairly. In short, there should be a sense of family in the department.

That is essentially what professors, both young and senior, told me at college after college when I was working on *Colleges That Change Lives*. Almost all of them had taught at elite universities, but had never experienced such collegiality or mutual respect and friendship in their departments. The professors' eyes had been opened to a new kind of world; their values and their lives had changed, just like their students'.

An assistant biology professor at Juniata sounded a common chord when he said, "One of the things that drew me to this place was collegiality." He and his colleagues might disagree, he said, but "we all respect what each other does." That sort of climate, he said, is more important than money: "If I'd been looking to get rich quick, I'd have gone to work in industry." An assistant professor of psychology at Juniata also spoke for many when she said the most important thing "is to feel valued and respected in your job." A young English professor at William Woods said the help and advice she gets from senior faculty members makes her feel "like I belong at this institution" and want "to invest back into the system. I would not trade for a $10,000 raise. Dollars don't necessarily make me feel valued."

She is not alone; many professors at good small colleges want to invest back into the system. They love teaching and seeing their students blossom. It is an act of love and passion. They do cutting-edge research as good as that of the university scholars, and inspire young collaborators and future scholars besides. The small college teachers are truly the nation's intellectual yeast, producing the next generation of scholars, scientists, and good citizens.

The universities, on the other hand, have become research institutes since *Sputnik*, and the attitude of many of their professors is "To hell with the undergraduate." Their goal is to achieve fame as scholars, not to invest back into the system or help freshmen or sophomores develop. As Dr. Katz of Princeton said, they aren't much good at liberal education and "are uncomfortable with values." The unwanted job of teaching is left to part-timers and assistants.

Few of them would merit the devotion of their students expressed over and over again by the good small college alumni. A former National Merit finalist was voicing the devotion of many across the country when he said ten years after graduating from Birmingham-Southern, "There are few things in life I am as grateful for as my experience at BSC. I miss it terribly. The English faculty contains some of the smartest, coolest, most wonderful professors ever to exist. Not only were they amazing instructors, they also became my friends."

The alumni at every college were sure they couldn't have had such amazingly brainy teachers or had their lives transformed so miraculously at any other institution, that their community was like no other.

A Hampshire alumna had a most revealing story of the high standards of rigor in the small college, and how much more revealing than grades are Hampshire's evaluations. She got an A+ on a paper at another of the Five Colleges (Amherst, Mount Holyoke, Smith, and the University of Massachusetts), but even before she got the grade, she'd thought how she could revise it and make it better. "The teacher," she said, "told me not to bother; I'd already gotten the A+. I'd done as well as possible according to this teacher's standards." She went on to graduate school and teaching college classes, where students whose papers were evaluated rather than graded developed into better writers.

It is a safe bet that I would not have gotten such euphoric testimony from university graduates.

CHAPTER 5

H *Is for Harvard and Hypocrisy,*
I *Is for "Ivy League Education"*

IF YOU WILL READ A stunningly revelatory book, *Excellence without a Soul: How a Great University Forgot Education*, by Dr. Harry R. Lewis, a Harvard faculty member for over thirty years and its dean for eight, you won't even look at Harvard or its clones. Why? Because the many Harvard sins and failures he details are the strengths of the good small college, the point I've been driving at for decades. The top universities, he says, have lost their way. They have become research institutes offering "hollow" education.

The purpose of education is to help teenagers find themselves and to make moral adults of them, Lewis argues. But Harvard and its clones, he says time and again, do neither. "Universities have lost their sense that their educational mission is to transform teenagers. They go to great lengths to make students happy, not better people," and the parents are complicit. They want their children's flaws hidden, not corrected. "Helicopter parents" also treat their children as they did at thirteen, rather than helping them become adults. He adds, "What students need most in this critical 18-to-22 period of development is help shaping the lives they, not their parents, will lead. This is when they find themselves and set ideals and objectives, but we seem oblivious." Lewis has been in many discussions over the years about the usual topics such as grades, curriculum, and student misdeeds, but "almost never about making students better people." The universities "lack confidence that they know what they're doing."

His first example is the 2002–4 effort to develop a new curriculum, of which he writes: "How could the Faculty of a great university talk for two years about the most basic questions of undergraduate education and come up with a curriculum consisting of empty bottles?" A member of the curriculum committee had said the group thought "the best thing to do was to put a row of empty bottles up there and see how the Faculty wanted to fill them."

Dr. Lewis fills 268 pages with the research university's sins and their causes.

The year before, in 2005, Dr. Katz of Princeton, had said liberal education in the research universities was so bad it threatened "the vitality of American democracy," but was "alive and well" in the good small colleges.

According to Dr. Lewis, "Harvard's leaders have allowed the school's mission to drift from education to consumer satisfaction. For them Harvard is no longer a city upon a hill but merely a brand name. . . . The old ideal of a liberal education lives on in name only . . . the whole educational experience does not cohere. Few could give a good answer, five or ten years after graduation day, to the simple question, 'What was the most important thing Harvard taught you?'"

Harvard, Lewis says, has been pursuing the wrong kind of excellence. Faculty are hired primarily for knowing more and more about less and less, and he quotes a publications editor as saying many scholarly books sell fewer than three hundred copies, one reason being that more and more "nonsense" is being published. The purpose of making students better people is not a factor, and teaching is only peripheral.

Lewis makes a point of saying that breadth of understanding, which may seem irrelevant, is just as important as depth of knowledge. It helps young students confront and solve their problems. He cites an example of a good student of his whose work was in a trough but who gave phony answers to questions in two conferences. Finally, the boy blurted out that his girlfriend was pregnant, and they hadn't told anyone. (Dr. Lewis, the friend and mentor, didn't explain what counsel or help he gave, but one assumes a solution was found.) But the universities have never decided what relationship faculty should have with undergraduates, and most of the faculty wants nothing to do with them.

We are still living with the aftershocks of an earthquake that happened more than a hundred years ago when colleges became universities. Indeed, the aftershocks are growing stronger, not weaker. Professors are hired as scholars and teachers, not as mentors of values and ideals to the young and confused. Instead of expecting professors to help students, universities hire counselors and advisors, and even take pride in absolving faculty of responsibility by touting peer advising systems that use students to do the job that professors should do.

Meanwhile, our official rhetoric continues to claim that the professors are the true source of guidance for students. For institutions that take pride in telling the truth, that hypocrisy is embarrassing.

Harvard's "cafeteria theory of education suggests that character and morality, fundamental standards onto which we hold when some turbulence dislodges the circumstances in our lives, are not the university's business at all." Some of the university's decisions are "unprincipled," and some professors would be bad role models for students, but Harvard does not punish the evildoers. Plagiarizing by law school professors—even a $26 million fraud of the government by a member of the economics department—has gone unpunished.

"It tiptoes away from moral education, little interested in providing it and embarrassed to admit it does not wish to do so." Lewis adds, "There is something wrong with our educational system when a majority of Harvard seniors go into consulting and investment banking as their best option for a productive life." Consultants have been named the villains in the collapse of Enron and Arthur Andersen, among others, for their lack of moral compasses. The late Kenneth Lay, head of Enron when it collapsed, had been a consultant himself.

Those "aftershocks" are getting worse, Lewis says, and will ultimately cause a rupture unless they are addressed with candor. Dr. Katz, though he did not go that far, has said there is little chance of the universities changing course, they have gone so far down the research road.

Harvard hires the best faculty, seeks the best students— and their interests have driven them apart. Faculty become more and more specialized and less and less interested in teaching what the students need, rather than what they want. But there is no competitive pressure to hire faculty who will help students become better people. The university has resorted to giving students all the amenities they want, even "beer halls on campus, and whatever the curricular complaint they respond by relaxing requirements so the students can do what they want to do." What the universities will not do, Lewis claims, is to place unsustainable demands on the professors, who are themselves free agents in a competitive market. "And the universities wonder why students are still unhappy. The students are unhappy because they want the faculty to be friends and mentors."

Dr. Lewis asks, What kind of leaders and citizens will Harvard, the trendsetter, be giving the nation when there is no effort to give them moral compasses, and what will be the consequences for the nation?

CHAPTER 6

Poison Ivy

Reprinted from the September 23, 2006,
issue of the *Economist*.

AMERICAN UNIVERSITIES LIKE TO THINK of themselves as
engines of social justice, thronging with "diversity." But how
much truth is there in this flattering self-image? Over the
past few years Daniel Golden has written a series of coruscat-
ing stories in the *Wall Street Journal* about the admissions
practices of America's elite universities, suggesting that they
are not so much engines of social justice as bastions of privilege. Now he has produced a book, *The Price of Admission:
How America's Ruling Class Buys Its Way into Elite Colleges—
and Who Get Left Outside the Gates*, that deserves to become
a classic.

Mr. Golden shows that elite universities do everything in
their power to admit the children of privilege. If they cannot
get them in through the front door by relaxing their standards,

then they smuggle them in through the back. No less than 60 percent of the places in elite universities are given to candidates who have some sort of extra "hook," from rich or alumni parents to "sporting prowess." The number of whites who benefit from this affirmative action is far greater than the number of blacks.

The American establishment is extraordinarily good at getting its children into the best colleges. In the 2004 presidential election, both candidates—George Bush and John Kerry—were C students who would have had little chance of getting into Yale if they had not come from Yale families. Two other prominent politicians both got their sons into their alma maters (Harvard and Princeton respectively) despite their average academic performances. Universities bend over backward to admit "legacies" (i.e., the children of alumni). Harvard admits 40 percent of legacy applicants compared with 11 percent of applicants overall. Amherst admits 50 percent. An average of 21 to 24 percent of students in each year at Notre Dame are the offspring of alumni. When it comes to the children of particularly rich donors, the bending-over-backward reaches astonishing levels. Harvard even has something called a "Z" list—a list of applicants who are given a place after a year's deferment to catch up— that is dominated by the children of rich alumni.

University behavior is at its worst when it comes to groveling to celebrities. Duke University's admissions director visited a very prominent Hollywood director's house to interview his stepdaughter. Princeton found a place for a model with family and political connections despite the fact that she had missed the application deadline by a month. Brown University was so keen to admit a well-known Hollywood deal maker's son that it gave him a place as a "special student." (He dropped out after a year.)

Most people think of black football and basketball stars when they hear about "sports scholarships." But there are also sports such as fencing, squash, sailing, riding, golf, and, of course, lacrosse. The University of Virginia even has scholarships for polo players, relatively few of whom come from the inner cities.

You might imagine that academics would be up in arms about this. Alas, they have too much skin in the game. Academics not only escape tuition fees if they can get their children into the universities where they teach, they get huge preferences as well. Boston University accepted 91 percent of "faculty brats" in 2003, at a cost of about $9 million. Notre Dame accepts about 70 percent of the children of university employees, compared with 19 percent of "unhooked" applicants, despite markedly lower average SAT scores.

Why do Mr. Golden's findings matter so much? The most important reason is that America is witnessing a potentially explosive combination of trends. Social inequality is rising at a time when the escalators of social mobility are slowing (America has lower levels of social mobility than most European countries). The returns on higher education are rising: the median earnings in 2000 of Americans with a bachelor's degree or higher were about double those of high school leavers. But elite universities are becoming more socially exclusive. Between 1980 and 1992, for example, the proportion of disadvantaged children in four-year colleges fell slightly (from 29 to 28 percent) while the proportion of well-to-do children rose substantially (from 55 to 66 percent).

Mr. Golden's findings do not account for all of this. Get rid of affirmative action for the rich, and rich children will still do better. But they clearly account for some differences: "unhooked" candidates are competing for just 40 percent of university places. And they raise all sorts of issues of justice and hypocrisy. What is one to make of a politician who opposes affirmative action for minorities while practicing it for his own child?

The Poor Left Behind

Two groups of people overwhelmingly bear the burden of these policies—Asian-Americans and poor whites. Asian-Americans are the "new Jews," held to higher standards (they need to score at least 50 points higher than non-Asians on the old SAT, even to be in the game) and frequently stigmatized for their "characters" (Harvard evaluators persistently rated Asian-Americans below whites on "personal qualities"). When the University of California at Berkeley briefly considered introducing means-based affirmative action, it rejected the idea on the ground that "using poverty yields a lot of poor white kids and poor Asian kids."

There are a few signs that the winds of reform are blowing. Several elite universities have expanded financial aid for poor children. Texas A&M has got rid of legacy preferences. In September 2006 Harvard announced that it was getting rid of its early admission program—a system that favors privileged children—and Princeton rapidly followed suit. But the wind is going to have to blow a heck of a lot harder, and for a heck of a lot longer, before America's money-addicted and legacy-loving universities can be shamed into returning to what ought to have been their guiding principle all along: admitting people to university on the basis of their intellectual ability.

CHAPTER 7

The Good College Experience: Growth

*The good college should train you for nothing and
prepare you for everything.*

—THE LATE BILL WILSON,
LONGTIME AMHERST ADMISSION DEAN

THE GOOD COLLEGE EXPERIENCE should disturb you, which
prepares you for growth. No pain, no gain. That was the un-
intended message of one of my first campus visits as education editor of the *New York Times*. I was at Amherst to
report on a new kind of college that could be replicated everywhere and thus solve the college-going panic of the
late 1950s.

The plan proposed by the four institutions in the area—
Amherst, Mount Holyoke, Smith, and the University of
Massachusetts—was to involve the student in his own education by way of research projects he proposed, rather than
lectures or discussion classes. Seven years later Hampshire,
which does just that and produces winners, was born.

On the same visit, quite different evidence of the good college experience was being unwittingly testified to in conversations with Amherst students, mostly freshmen. Many of them were disturbed; having won admission to one of the country's most selective colleges, they were asking what they were doing there, what they were being prepared for, what the object of the enterprise was. They could see no specific roles for themselves after graduation, especially if they hadn't made a firm choice of major.

They were neither the first nor the last college freshmen to feel that way. But at a big university, such questions would have been less likely. The students there would probably have felt safely on track in their vocationally oriented programs. If the Amherst students had taken their apprehensions to Bill Wilson, the man who had admitted them, he could have assured them that Amherst knew what it was doing, and that if their college experience didn't disturb them, especially in their sophomore year, something was the matter.

So would many others in and out of the academic world, from Aristotle on. They would have made two points: one, that the student should be involved in his own education for it to be effective; and two, that the experience should teach him to think and should work its way into his values, and that will be a disturbing process.

John Stuart Mill said that a man is a man before he is a physician or a philosopher or a plumber, and that if you make him a reasonable and sensible man, he'll make himself a reasonable and sensible physician or philosopher or plumber. Yale had the same idea about the same time. In 1828 it announced that its undergraduates would get no professional courses because nothing was as practical as good theory or as useful as a liberal education. Professional studies, they said, could come later.

Vocational preparation, whether for engineering, medicine, business, or plumbing, is concerned with the job rather than the person. It does not seek to achieve the liberating and enlightening changes in values, attitudes, and thinking that will help a student lead a productive and fulfilling life. That is only done by way of a liberal education. The vocational route prepares for only the most temporary of temporal satisfactions: the first job. Almost everybody changes jobs in the first years after graduation. And who has a crystal ball clear enough to see his last job? The fact is that for this and coming generations, the odds are overwhelming that it hasn't been invented yet.

In a commencement address as outgoing dean at Indiana University, Dr. John Lombardi said, "College teaches us the skills for success at any job. When we hear the refrain, 'How come I don't have a job on the day I graduate from college?' we are sympathetic but not overly concerned. Practically all of us are doing things we like to do and want to within five years after graduation."

Liberal arts graduates twenty and twenty-five years out of school invariably testify that it was the attitudes and ways of thinking, not the specific courses or information they got in college, that contributed to their success. This has been the experience of such colleges as Oberlin, Haverford, and Amherst when they polled their graduates in mid-career. These unusually successful men and women claimed in overwhelming numbers that the liberal arts path was what did it for them. If they had to do it over again they would take more courses in the arts, humanities, and sciences.

The liberal arts message, however, is seldom heard by the high school student who hasn't a chance of getting into an Amherst, the kind of place he envisions as guaranteeing a good job and a successful career. His worries are more acute. If—lacking the perceived leverage of a brand-name school—he doesn't know what he wants to major in and what kind of job he should be thinking about, he often thinks he is imperiling his future.

I have tried to reassure many of these students that not only are they not failures, but neither their own parents nor most of the successful people in this country had any idea at age eighteen of what they would be doing at age fifty. If they once thought they did, nine of out ten turned out to be wrong, because those nine wound up in jobs that had nothing whatever to do with their original college majors, and they were glad of it; they were happy in what they were doing because both they and the world had grown and changed.

When I made this point at a meeting with seniors at the best prep school in Washington, one boy asked incredulously, "You mean just major in the liberal arts?" So far as he was concerned, I was trying to put him in a boat without an engine, sail, or rudder.

When the job market got dismally soft in the 1970s, parents were more of a problem than the teenagers. More than once a father said, "Look at this boy; he's a real problem. He's eighteen years old and has no idea what he wants to do." It almost always turned out during the subsequent interview that the father hadn't known what he wanted to do either, when he was that age.

As John L. Munschauer, Cornell University's longtime career-development service director, put it, "Thirty years in college placement have taught me that the future is uncertain. Choosing a major by trying to outguess the job market is like speculating on corn futures." His words were common knowledge except to teenagers, and the proof of the pudding was a poll that could have been taken forty years earlier or today, with the same results. This is it:

The University of Virginia, where most of the students think they are safely locked into career tracks—as do those at most universities—published a 1984 survey of its College of Arts and Sciences graduates three to thirteen years out of school to prove that there is, as the booklet is titled, "Life after Liberal Arts." In an effort to educate high school students and their parents, the College of Arts and Sciences asked two thousand alumni who had graduated between 1971 and 1981 what their jobs and salaries were and whether their liberal arts background had been an asset or a liability. Young professionals of all kinds gave the same emphatic answers as have alumni of several liberal arts colleges in other such polls: a liberal arts education was responsible for their success; it had proven to be the most practical and useful. Hardly any of the Virginia alumni were in jobs that had any obvious connection with their college majors, or even with their first-time jobs. Eighty-five percent of them were satisfied in their jobs, and 91 percent said they would recommend a liberal arts degree to undergraduates considering the same careers.

Not only were they working in twenty-four different areas that covered the waterfront, but many of them have had five or six jobs since graduation. One, a marketing manager of American Cyanamid Co., had had eight, and a Chase Manhattan Bank vice president six. The median salary was $30,000. Fourteen percent earned $60,000 or more, and 21 percent earned $50,000 or more. These salary figures are in 1984 dollars.

Their jobs included legislative aide to Senator Daniel Patrick Moynihan; a special assistant to the president; senior editor, *Money* magazine; executive director, American Bankers Association; president of a computer systems firm; and lighting designer, Atlanta Ballet—and not one of these six had majored in his field.

Whether they were in systems analysis, television sales forecasting, network editorial production, electronics, or medicine, these very successful young people offered teenagers, and especially their parents, the same advice: stop thinking of college as a four-year ticket to a lucrative job in this or that profession; it doesn't work that way in the real world.

Hardly any of these men and women found it easy to get the first job. They had to work at it, and they experienced all the discouragement, uncertainty, and confusion that liberal arts graduates often complain of. Moreover, five out of six of them hadn't been happy in their first jobs, and within three years, three out of four had changed jobs.

But now they say with almost one voice that college should provide an education that teaches one to think and to solve problems, to write and speak effectively, to work with people, and to gain a broad view of the world. These "liberal arts" skills, they say, may not make it any easier to get the first job, but they are what really matter once a person starts moving up through the ranks.

Eighty percent of the Virginia alumni said that what employers valued most were not the grades, the major, or the graduate degrees, but rather personal characteristics, chief of which were enthusiasm, ability to relate to others, and ability to work independently.

The specific skills they have found most important include oral and written communication, interpersonal skills, problem solving, and critical thinking. The owner of a business consulting firm who had been an English major said, "Communication skills are critical. My ability to analyze the Internal Revenue Code is the same skill as analyzing a poem or short story." The vice president of a graphics design firm said, "After ten years I've just realized what I really learned at UVa, unbeknownst to me while it was happening—i.e., how to think and solve problems. This is the single most important factor in my current success."

In the soft job market of the late 1970s, employers said pretty much the same things to three different colleges that had obtained grants to find out from corporate, industrial, and government employers what made a college graduate attractive to them. Invariably, the employers said it was the ability to communicate with the written and the spoken word, which means being able to think; attitude toward work; and having the respect of peers. These were far more important than what so many college students consider the holy trinity: major, grade point average, and name of institution.

One-third of the Virginia alumni believed their liberal arts training had given them an advantage over their colleagues, while another one-third felt their careers would have proceeded no differently had they pursued a technical degree.

A business analyst with GTE Telenet Communications who was an English major and who later got a master of business administration degree said, "I was not able to find a career job until after graduating from business school. However, I now find that my English literature degree gives me a definite advantage over those who have strictly business or technical degrees."

The high school senior who has his mind set on a business major should listen to one of the Virginia alums, a bank vice president now but a biology major in college. He said, "A liberal arts background provided me with an overall understanding of people, politics, and society, which are most important to the understanding of marketing." This is his third job. His first one was as a $7,200-a-year junior high school teacher.

A big reason for these students' success, which shines through their answers and the advice they give, is initiative. They tell students to get involved in campus activities, but for substance, not for show; to take some career-related courses, to get internships and have summer work experiences, and finally, to use initiative in investigating career possibilities and in looking for an actual job. Eighty-six percent of them said their own personal initiative was crucial to their being hired for their first job.

The Virginia results, like all similar polls, destroy any basis for one of the most persistent and harmful myths about college; namely, that when you choose a major, you're choosing your career. The reality is that there is virtually no connection between liberal arts majors and future career paths. But in spite of continuing, unarguable proof to the contrary, students and their parents persist in wearing the job-track blinders.

Perhaps the person who takes the liberal arts route is more venturesome, more intellectually curious, and has more get-up-and-go than the one who is seeking safety in the job track. The liberal arts graduate has to sell himself more than the one with the professional degree, and this makes him more alert, juices up his adrenaline, and activates the imagination and gray cells. It stimulates his survival instincts, teaches him to land on his feet, and makes him a better performer and competitor.

MIT's engineering dean evinced such thoughts when, in announcing that the technical school's undergraduates were going to get a lot more exposure to the elements of liberal education, she said, "Too many MIT graduates wind up working for too many Harvard, Yale, and Princeton graduates."

I have boasted for years that I could be dropped blindfolded onto any engineering campus in the United States, with the possible exceptions of Caltech and Harvey Mudd, and in less than half an hour know it was an engineering school. Few students or faculty will be interested in what's going on in the world or on campus. Once, at Carnegie-Mellon, walking down a hall of the newest and most distinctive building on campus, I asked in five successive faculty offices who the architect was. When the fifth one didn't know and I observed that it was the only new and different building around, his reply was, "We tend not to think in those terms." I said, "Don't you think you ought to?"

Faculty members so barren of aesthetic or intellectual curiosity are not likely to contribute much of value outside the tricks and techniques of their trades. This single-track mind-set is one reason that in engineering's lean years engineers have so much trouble finding jobs. They have trouble adapting because their preparation has fitted them with blinders.

A dramatic example of how the liberal arts' broad exposures can enable a person to find his true love—or, more precisely, to see that one's current love may really be collateral preparation for the real thing—is the story of one of the ablest and most intellectual persons of any age I have ever known. He was also the only client or friend from whom I ever received a letter with a paragraph of Aristotle's *Ethics* in Greek pasted on the back of the envelope, with his translation below it.

An omnivorous reader, he had always considered himself betrothed to the classics and saw himself as headed for a career as a classics professor, which was his ideal of the rewarding life: being a source of intellectual stimulation and passing on the heritage of civilization. Furthermore, a professor at Chicago had told him in his freshman year that he was good enough to get the one classics vacancy that might exist in academia when he got his PhD. But like other intelligent youths, he had catholic interests: Dorothy Sayers's detective novels, theories of education, tennis, swimming, and art; he was a frequent visitor to Washington's galleries.

He didn't like Chicago and transferred to Oberlin as a sophomore, where two disturbing things happened—as they are likely to in a good college. He was only two semesters away from a major in Greek when he discovered William Blake, the English artist and poet, and did a paper on him. Second, he fell under the spell of a wonderful teacher who awakened a sleeping passion. Late in his junior year, he wrote me:

Today I had the extreme pleasure of visiting Ellen Johnson [Oberlin art history professor emeritus] in her beautiful Frank Lloyd Wright home. She is a charming and inspirational woman who overflows with life and love, and her house is so wonderful. It was one of the most inspiring one and a half hours I've ever spent. I only wish I could have taken a class from her. At the beginning she said something that I've always believed, that scholarship and teaching are acts of love, and went on to prove this, for when she gave a tour of her home and art collection and pointed to a [painting by] Rauschenberg or Dine or Jasper Jones, et al., all the people who had been troubling me lately, and said, "Isn't it lovely," I had no doubts.

The fact that he now has his doctorate in art history, after having had his pick of all the richest and most prestigious fellowships, testifies not only to his abilities but also to the fact that he had the good experience that affects a person's life by helping him find the route he wants to take. He will still be pursuing his goal of passing on the heritage of civilization, but it will be by way of art rather than by way of Greek and Roman literature. And he will be a more broad-gauge, perceptive art historian for having the classics background.

His experience stands out like a city of gold compared with that of another client, a girl from a New York City suburb who made a wrong choice, then transferred after a year. She wrote,

I had no focused idea of exactly what "being educated" entailed. My father had graduated from Hamilton College, and my older sister was completing her junior year there. . . . I chose not to attend Hamilton and accepted a place at Indiana University solely on the basis of its size (24,000 undergraduates) and its location. . . . Going to a large school in the Midwest would be an interesting and exciting experience. . . . I wanted to strike out into new territory.

Having spent almost one full academic year at Indiana University has helped me learn more about myself . . . and what kind of education I want. . . . The size of Indiana University, although one of the primary reasons I chose the school, has often been the cause of great frustration to me. Three out of my four classes have well over 100 students in them, which gives rise to little or no interaction between the professor and the students. I dislike the lack of give and take in the classroom. At Hamilton, a class of 20 instead of 200 gives everyone a chance to raise questions and state opinions. . . . Simply taking notes in a lecture hall and spitting them back on the exam leaves little room for growth as a student. . . . At Hamilton I can have a greater chance to get to know my professor, and he or she will know me as more than simply a Social Security number.

Students at a school as large as Indiana often do not feel part of the community. My dorm alone has over 2,000 people living in it, and I sometimes feel that I am living in an apartment building in a large city rather than on a college campus. Although I know a lot of people to say "Hi" to on my way to and from classes, for the most part my friendship with them is on a very superficial basis.

I would like to become involved in as many different activities in college as I was in high school. At Indiana it is almost impossible to become involved in acting unless one is a theater major, or to work on the *Indiana Daily Student* unless one is a journalism major, or to join the women's track team unless one had record-breaking times in high school. I miss my extracurricular activities.

It is with great regret that I have found that I am not interested in the same subjects that most of my classmates are. . . . I am in the school of liberal arts and they are in the school of business. The Business School at Indiana attracts renowned professors as well as highly motivated students. English and the humanities are, on the whole, considered of a lesser caliber than business courses. The students taking English courses tend to be either fulfilling a requirement or hoping for an easy A (and are often disappointed). I have found few friends who truly love the liberal arts, and while they must be there, I have not found them. I would look forward to being at a school like Hamilton where the humanities and English are truly valued, and where I could be in class with others who feel about them as I do.

She did transfer to Hamilton, where she found more of the shared values she wanted, and which are an essential ingredient of the good college experience. An engineer is not going to be happy in the Great Books program at St. John's College in Annapolis unless he's interested in ideas as well as how things work. An artistic Bennington or a venturesome Hampshire student is going to feel strangely out of place in a technical Lehigh or Rensselaer, and vice versa.

A sense of shared values is one mark of a good college, just as it is of a good high school. The inspiring success of an inner-city high school in Richmond, Virginia, in providing an escape hatch from the ghetto for poor kids has been, like others in other cities, a story of shared values. Students and parents made a compact that stipulated four years each of a foreign language, math, and science, in addition to English, history, government, computer science, passing the Red Cross swimming test, and doing community service. The parents agreed to provide study space and quiet for the required two hours of daily study. Every single member of the graduating class went on to college. And they went to Princeton, Duke, Oberlin, Rice, Howard, and Virginia Military Institute, among others. Had it not been for Richmond Community High School, a few of them might have gone to the local community college. The colleges most likely to affect a person's growth operate on the same principle of shared values.

If more parents and teenagers had been reading some of the serious studies of the good small colleges, such as *Changing Values in College*, by Philip Jacob, or *The Distinctive College*, by Burton R. Clark, many college choices would have been more wisely made. These two books, among others, show that the colleges that turn out people who accomplish things and who make contributions are places that hold in common values of ethical integrity and of service. They are places with a sense of mission.

They could also have profited from reading Nicholas von Hoffman's *Megaversity*, for a depressing portrayal of the routine rite of passage that is the lot of the great majority in the universities who aren't good enough students or fortunate enough to be in some special program. It is a routine in which the student has little interest or involvement in anything beyond getting the degree.

The good colleges have a commitment to learning, meaning work; high expectations for both students and faculty; a strong sense of purpose; and a sense of community. Haverford College, which has as productive and successful a body of alumni as any, has conducted exit interviews of its graduating seniors for many years to get reactions to their four years there. One of the threads that runs through these interviews is the students' feeling of a strong sense of community. Another, attributable to its honor code, which is both social and academic, is that "trust is the rule." The college seniors say also that Haverford gave them values.

These graduates also have something to say to high school seniors who think they must go to a college larger than their high school in order to have an adequate social and learning experience, a fixation that seems to afflict at least half the young people I talk to. After four years in a school of one thousand students, the Haverford seniors don't think it's too small. College has been for them a time of internal exploration, and the small community is more conducive to that than the large one.

Since Haverford students are not only very intelligent but tend to be more self-sufficient than most, they may more readily appreciate why virtually every good college in the country is smaller than most suburban high schools. Virtually every good college is around two thousand or under for a reason: involvement, something that is hard to come by in the big university. In their college visits, a team headed by

Ernest L. Boyer for the Carnegie Foundation for the Advancement of Teaching's book *College: The Undergraduate Experience in America*, only 20 percent of the liberal arts college students did not feel a sense of community, whereas overall, 40 percent did not.

Involvement is crucial. Alexander Astin of the University of California at Los Angeles, who has been studying the effects of college on students for thirty years, says small colleges have a greater positive impact on students than large ones, and private ones more than public ones. The small ones rate higher in student achievement than the big ones, and the key is student involvement, both in campus life and in learning.

In gathering evidence for their book, Dr. Boyer's team came to much the same conclusions after talking to five thousand students at all kinds of institutions: "We conclude that the effectiveness of the undergraduate experience . . . is directly linked to the time students spend on campus and to the quality of their involvement in activities." Honors programs and undergraduate research programs are also central to productive experiences.

The outstanding records in producing scientists made by fifty small colleges offer some proof. The small colleges dramatically outperformed twenty leading universities, and the key was student involvement in their own education, in this case by way of collaborative student-faculty research.

Dr. Boyer's team documented with some damning statistics the differences between what is likely to be a good personal experience in a small college and the relatively uncaring and impersonal process of the university. They found that few university faculty members carry even half a normal college teaching load. Indeed, at the research universities, 61 percent teach only one to four hours a week or none at all, and at the doctorate-granting institutions, 38 percent had little or no contact with undergraduates. Moreover, as he quoted Harvard sociologist David Riesman, "their commitment to research can have a chilling effect on the classroom and be shockingly detrimental to students." The undergraduate is an unwanted, often rejected or merely tolerated child.

At the liberal arts colleges, 85 percent of the faculty polled by Dr. Boyer's team were interested primarily in teaching, as opposed to 39 percent in the research universities and 60 percent in the public universities. As might be expected, half again as many liberal arts as university students said their professors were interested in their academic progress or encouraged them to discuss their feelings about important issues. Better than nine out of ten liberal arts college students said their professors encouraged discussion in class.

It would have been man-bites-dog news if Dr. Boyer's team had found anything different. Colleges make bragging points of having small classes and professors who love to teach. And good teachers like discussion; it demands mental activity by the student. In fact, one university professor told Dr. Boyer's people that if his own undergraduate math classes had been as large as the one he was teaching, he would never have become a mathematician. In short, the undergraduate is far more likely to get only half a loaf in the university, and the classroom half he does get has a short shelf life.

Involvement means the college provides opportunities for department seminars, tutorials, student research programs, opportunities for interdisciplinary and independent study, jointly taught courses, close collaboration between teachers and the library, and senior theses. These are some of the things that mark the good college experience and that should be asked about when a student visits the school.

Today, off-campus programs, which weren't widely available in the 1950s, provide many exciting ways of making the student an active participant. They cover almost every conceivable interest and are scattered around the globe. The twenty-five members of the Associated Colleges of the Midwest (ACM) and the Great Lakes Colleges Association (GLCA), for example, offer study semesters in Africa, India, Japan, Hong Kong, Latin America, Scotland, and Yugoslavia. There are arts programs in New York, Florence, London, and elsewhere. There are internships of all kinds that provide professional experience and that often lead to jobs after graduation.

Students with interests in the sciences or social sciences can be part of research teams at the Oak Ridge and Argonne national laboratories. At ACM's Wilderness Field Station in the headwaters of the Mississippi in northern Minnesota, students can paddle and portage for two weeks studying animal and plant habitats. Others can intern in local governments, doing urban studies in Chicago or Philadelphia, or in Holland or Yugoslavia if they prefer.

Consortia such as these offer students a variety of off-campus experiences cooperatively that one college couldn't afford to do alone. In the New York arts program, for example, fifty students from the twelve GLCA schools work as apprentices or interns with playwrights and sculptors, as subcurators in museums, as assistant stage managers in off-Broadway productions, or as interns in architectural firms, among others, getting hands-on experience.

They gather regularly at their Upper West Side headquarters, where a mostly ad hoc faculty works with them and where they compare notes and evaluate their experiences. When they return to their campuses, their schoolwork has a new meaning, and a valuable experience has been added, whether or not they ever become artists or architects or curators. About half the students in the twenty-five colleges have spent a study term or a year abroad or elsewhere off campus by the time they graduate, many times the figure nationwide.

These are only two examples of the many consortium arrangements across the country that broaden the offerings of individual colleges. Some are more workable than others. The Five Colleges consortium of Amherst, Hampshire, Mount Holyoke, Smith, and the University of Massachusetts is a prime example of one that does work. Students can take classes at any other institution, and some courses are joint enterprises. Synchronized calendars and class scheduling and a free minibus system that runs at frequent intervals make it practicable, and over nine thousand students a year take courses on other campuses. They really do have at their disposal the resources of four other institutions.

But consortium arrangements aside, virtually every good college has some off-campus and overseas programs, or will help the student make arrangements for them and provide leaves of absence for internships or a term on another campus. There is a general acceptance of these things that did not exist a few decades ago. For many students, taking a term away from school for an internship in a government agency or a business has been one of the most valuable parts of their college experience. And some mention such experience first when talking about their college days.

Antioch College has offered an exceptional education program since 1921. There, students spend alternate quarters in campus study periods and on jobs. Or, they may have creative study projects off campus or participate in a GLCA overseas program. Antioch believes, and so do its alumni (who as a group are among the most successful and productive of all), that if the purpose of college is to help people become independent beings, off-campus jobs and projects are essential.

Antioch students, like Haverford's, tend to know who they are and to be self-sufficient human beings—in fact, they do Haverford's one better. I've never encountered a student body as independent and uppity, or as involved, anywhere. The students have a voice in the governance of the college, and they exercise it. A meeting on cafeteria prices, which might have drawn a half-dozen students at many colleges, attracted two rooms jammed full there. And the student chairman told the food service managers, "Now, Jack, we're not asking for answers; we're demanding them."

In short, what has been working for Antioch students for almost a century is now enriching the experiences of countless others, if on a much more modest scale.

In the past, when Antioch was having one of its three financial crises of the twentieth century, I would assure parents that if the crisis was really life-threatening, some foundation would come to the rescue, because this country could not afford not to have an Antioch. I said Antioch was the yeast of American higher education, tiny but mighty in its effect. The time has come to prevent a national tragedy: Antioch's board of trustees, lacking funds to maintain a 100-acre campus and its adjoining 1,000-acre nature preserve, has decided to close the campus temporarily but keep the many Antioch University satellite institutions and the Antioch degree intact, with plans to open the campus anew in 2012. Hope can be a main ingredient of the best of plans, but meanwhile what teenagers want is a main campus, with its many attractions and its central focus. To do this, and to restore a healthy Antioch, the board needs money, lots of it.

A central ingredient on the college's side is rigor. If it's easy, it's a sham. It's a fun task to find out how rigorous a place is and what its standards are just by asking a couple dozen students and two or three of the faculty. The students will be eager to talk, and most faculty members are stoop-shouldered with honesty and will level with the questioner, even though they work there.

One might assume the more famous or prestigious the school, the more rigorous it is. Not necessarily. How demanding a school is and how much active learning is going on are matters that have a whole lot less to do with prestige than most college shoppers think. A few years ago, a young friend who had been at Princeton a year and a half and then transferred wrote me, "I am finding Macalester very satisfactory. The level of teaching is as high as it was at Princeton, at least in my experience, and one must work about as hard to keep up." And a girl who transferred to Beloit in Wisconsin from prestigious Wesleyan in Connecticut said the difference to her was a cold feeling of every person for himself at the Little Ivy.

But rigor is central to the quality of a school, large or small. A girl who transferred from East Carolina University— a school that was made a university by legislative fiat—to the University of Wisconsin wrote, "All of my classes are so much more stimulating. It isn't even fair to compare them with the ones at my other school. My grades are good; not all As, like at East Carolina, but I'm sure I'll be more proud of whatever grades I earn because I've worked very hard."

Two of the criteria I use in recommending colleges are a predominantly residential student body, and a sizable proportion of students from outside the college's immediate region. The second is less important than the first. Knox College, a grade-A school by any measure, has slightly over 40 percent out-of-state students, but it has a cosmopolitan student body, heavily from the Chicago metropolitan area, and more Illinois Scholars than any college in the state.

Kalamazoo in Michigan is another gem that if it were on the East Coast would be as selective as any other college and a lot better than its neighbors, whatever state it was in. Like Knox, most of its students are from its area, but few colleges have as distinguished a record of producing graduates who go on to get doctorates or achieve mention in *Who's Who*. Some teenagers are put off by the name, but Kalamazoo is a most attractive city.

The residential character of a college, however, is far more important than the geographical distribution of its student body; it is vital. Without it, there can hardly be much sense of community; the experience will be more like an extension of high school. It is much more difficult to either establish or maintain any real student-faculty friendships at a commuter school. And since commuters leave after class, there is no sense of community, no likelihood of shared values or sense of mission.

Wherever a student goes to college, it is absolutely essential that she become a participating member of that community. People who are involved get more out of anything, whether it's college or life, and they are the ones who don't drop out. Every data-gatherer who's done a study has found this to be true. Dr. Alexander Astin, whose work has been the most comprehensive, says flatly that this is a fact of life. And in thirty years on and off campus, I can't recall an unhappy or dissatisfied student who was an involved one.

That is not to say that there aren't good and sufficient reasons for wanting to transfer. The student may have made a bad choice, or some special programs or major or ten thousand more people may make another place more alluring. However, transferring to get some specialized major is more often than not a poor idea. Unless a person is an absolute whiz in some field such as physics, which has many specialties, he's going to get all he can carry away in any good college.

When a person wants to transfer from a grade-A college like Grinnell to Boston University, as one girl I know did, she is sacrificing most of the quality of her college for a mess of bigger population pottage. When someone says there's nothing to do or that there's no social life, it usually means she hasn't made any effort and hasn't gotten involved. Also, if she says that everyone knows too much about you in a small college, she is missing the point. Or she may want something less troublesome than an education.

Lack of involvement is the reason commuter and part-time students as a group get so much less out of college. They're not a part of the family; they just come to class and go home. Usually there are no meeting places or activities especially for them. And since they're not around for the regular campus activities and cultural or social events, they don't have the benefit of the out-of-class contacts that the residential students do. Consequently, they don't get to know their professors or their classmates as well as they could. So it isn't surprising that, living on the fringe, they are much more likely to drop out. Furthermore, they are much less likely to go on to graduate school.

The shortcomings of the commuter student's experience are worth talking about because parents often are tempted to send a child who hasn't performed well in high school to a nearby community college for a year to prove herself. They say that it's only the first year, after all, and she can have the other three away at college. The troubles with this approach are two: One, the freshman year is at least as important as the other three, probably more so. Two, the community college is likely to be an extension of high school; just as distracting, with all the same temptations, and in the company of others for most of whom those two years will be the end of the educational line.

Most of the teenagers at community colleges are not much involved, either academically or in college life. It is the mature students for whom the community colleges are a godsend and who tend to get the most out of what they offer. It requires more than the normal endowment of moral fiber for a teenager to make himself work hard under those circumstances. It is a much better bet to have the student start at a residential college—with luck, one where there is a good learning atmosphere. Not only will the residential college very likely be more stimulating, but living with others who have some interest in learning and achieving is more likely to rub off. The most important single everyday influence is a good, studious roommate. That kind is a lot more conducive to good habits than one who says, "Let's go to a movie," or "Let's go have a beer." Next, obviously, is the kind of group a student associates with.

The perils of bad roommates notwithstanding, it is important that the student live in the dorms if possible. Simply because they're living right there on the grounds and are part of the scene—unlike students living in apartment houses in town, whose attention is likely to be focused elsewhere—they're much more likely to be involved in two of the requisites of a good experience: a continuing conversation with teachers, who, aside from the library, are the learning resources of the place; and a continuing conversation with fellow students.

That the condition of most dormitory rooms reflects the fact that most teenagers are slobs should not deter parents, however appalled they may be. Thirty years ago, their own college rooms were surely just as bad. In the days when coed dorms were still in their infancy, the columnist Art Buchwald visited the college where his youngest daughter was a freshman. I happened to have visited there a couple of weeks earlier, and thought that even given how unkempt most dorm rooms were, those were awful messes.

Speaking at a convocation, Mr. Buchwald said, "I've had a tour of your campus and I've been through your dorms. And after seeing them, it's not sex in the dorms I'm worried about; it's cholera."

Many years ago, the *Oberlin Review* carried an article by Sally Brown, a Williams student who was spending her junior year at Oberlin. That article is a good way to end this chapter because it is still true, and it adroitly draws some differences between two colleges (which both colleges would say are overdrawn), their students, and their involvement.

A PLACE TO COME TO

I hate coming to new places. I never went to sleep away at camp; at least that was the rationalization I used freshman year. I had skipped a year and never gone away for the summer, that's why I hated college. How could I hate college? Seven thousand a year and I had the audacity to hate it.

I went to Williams College in Massachusetts, not the one in Virginia. Actually, I still go there. I am what you would call a "visiting student." Why did I come to Oberlin? I know I need a quick, pat reply. You have to remember that it is unusual to spend junior year abroad forty minutes out of Cleveland.

When I first got to Williams I couldn't believe how pretty it was. It was beautiful and the people were really nice. My "junior adviser's" name was Mary. She had on these amazing pants, red corduroys. This is before Fiorucci started selling them.

First we all went to the semiformal banquet. Everybody put on skirts or suits. We went to the gym and heard speeches. Then the kegs. Every floor of every dorm had a keg and unlike Keep Co-op, people finished them. Everybody was amazed at how diverse I was, coming from

New York and all. They couldn't believe I had come out alive. Or that I didn't play tennis. At 18 I realized I was "counterculture." By junior year I was beginning to believe that I was a revolutionary.

I decided to come to Oberlin, to put Williams into perspective, and maybe to see if I actually had some revolutionary potential. I don't. The guy across the hall had the audacity to call me preppie. He said he could picture me as a Madison Avenue executive. What does he know, anyway?

I showed him when my friend George Rivers Wilbanks, Jr. came to visit me. He was driving home for break in his new car. He had an Audi but got bored with it. Now he has a baby blue Impala. He calls her Motown.

He stocked the Dennet house beer machine at Williams. He thought this place was WILD. The co-op was UNBELIEVABLE. Riv went to the Disco. Claims he talked to gay men. Even danced with one of them. WOW. They knew he was straight though. They saw him staring at the women, WILD. He didn't like the beer.

Freshmen at Williams live only with freshmen of their own sex. They usually have singles. Freshmen at Oberlin use bathrooms open to all classes and sexes. They always have doubles. Williams has Homecoming Weekend equipped with semiformal dances with a victorious football team. Oberlin has Mayfair and the Harkness Night Club. When Williams men want to score they road-trip up to Skidmore. Oberlin women are aware of their bodies and go to Wilder to buy specula.

At Oberlin people want to find themselves. At Williams such angst is unheard of. Everybody at Oberlin has lived on a kibbutz. Everybody at Williams has met a Jew, usually during their freshman year. Williams students have direction. There are markets to be conquered. Oberlin students see contradictions. There are people to be helped. When Williams students cite tradition it usually means the Republican party. When Oberlin students call forth tradition it usually means progressive action. The Williams liberal political club graduated last year. The Oberlin Moderate Caucus has six members.

This is not to say that Oberlin is utopian or that Williams is hellish. They're just different extremes. They produce different stereotypes. In both cases you find closet moderates.

The Williams stereotype is the career-oriented 90th-generation American blond-haired business type who plays a wicked game of squash.

The Oberlin stereotype is the guilt-ridden, second-generation American brown-haired type with no idea of what they will be doing in five years but may be traveling in the interim.

Introspection is key here. In the past few months I've come to terms with more personal problems than I ever knew I had. One thing is good, I know I'm not being selfish when I talk about these things. It's very important to externalize, you know. Also better for eavesdropping, particularly in the Snack Bar. You find more libidos there than any place else on campus, or in Ohio, for that matter.

Yes, I like Oberlin better than Williams. No, I haven't worked as hard but that could be my courses. Yes, the people are wonderful. No, the landscape doesn't inspire me. No, I'm not going to transfer. It would be very complicated and I'd end up having to spend an extra semester in college. Also Williams is a little better for my career interests.

Here are two great schools and two dramatically different impacts. As this little parody illustrates, the good experience may be very different for different people. And that leads us to the next step: select, don't settle.

CHAPTER 8

Select, Don't Settle

DESPITE THE HIGH-BLOOD-PRESSURE anxiety that has been getting families closer to nervous collapses every year, you can select your college, and a better one than the designer-label ones your peers are sweating and fretting for. You can even have choices. That assumes, of course, that what you want is an intellectually demanding four years that may change or lift your aspirations and empower you to achieve them.

This is not what most people want. Some are feverish for the designer-label diploma, which they mistakenly think is the union card for the first job or to become a doctor, lawyer, or economist and lead the good life.

A lot are going just for the degree, any degree, or because it was the thing expected of them, or because they can have a four-year, all-expenses-paid free ride, courtesy of Mom and Pop.

You, however, can select from some of the best in the country if you work at it and look beyond the Ivy and its clones. But first you must do the self-examination in chapter 10. Follow Aristotle's injunction to "know thyself"—otherwise it's a pig-in-a-poke business.

The Ivies and their clones are not the best bets. As Judge Gladys Kessler said of the tobacco industry in her landmark racketeering decision in 2006, the research universities have been lying and deceiving the public about the quality of their undergraduate education for decades. In 2005, a prominent Ivy scholar detailed their failings, which are described in chapter 1, "Twenty-one Myths That Can Jinx Your College Choice."

His exposé was several decades overdue. When university teaching faculty topped 43 percent part-timers, even the cautious Department of Education had to take note, commenting that the situation "threatens the validity of the university as a teaching institution." In the late 1950s, Dr. Harry Gideonse, president of Brooklyn College, said, "If the Federal Trade Commission ever started prosecuting colleges [and universities] for false and misleading advertising, there'd be more college than corporate presidents under cease and desist orders."

The famous scholars the universities boast of do little, if any, teaching and practically no advising. They are only name performers behind a lectern. But in good small colleges the teacher is a mentor, an adviser, and a friend. In some casual chat he may strike the spark that changes your life. In other words, what happens outside class can be more important than what happens in class.

Name-brand schools reject more A students than they accept. However, nearly 80 percent of all students are in their first-choice colleges. In no other country does a teenager have such a plethora of choices (more than 2,000 four-year institutions) to confuse the issue or encourage so many frivolous choices with such costly consequences. Most choices are so badly made that only about three in ten freshmen are on the same campuses four years later.

The search doesn't have to involve a great number of schools, but it does require that Aristotle's injunction be the first order of business, followed by a lot of pick and shovel work informing yourself about the colleges. Use the Internet! Next, visits are essential, to quiz faculty members and students about the school's claims and about the things important to you.

It is important when you visit a college to take a hard-nosed consumer attitude—not "Am I good enough for this school?" but "Is this school good enough for me?" Even with more kids going to college, there are always other schools just as good or better, even if you haven't heard of them. (Besides, the Department of Education has been way off on several other forecasts, including a terrible faculty shortage.)

Most of the academic bargains will be in the hundreds of good small liberal arts colleges, including those in the companion book to this one, *Colleges That Change Lives*, which may solve your problems. The small college comes closest to the old Dartmouth definition of the good education: Mark Hopkins on one end of a log and the student on the other.

For the able student who wants to do honors work and, unlike most teenagers, can accept responsibility for working on his own, New College in Florida offers a different kind of choice. Unlike St. John's College in Annapolis or Santa Fe, where the curriculum is fixed, or Reed, where there is a core of required courses, the 700 students at New College make contracts for what they propose to do, and there are no required courses. There are, however, three independent study projects, a senior thesis, and an oral defense of it before a faculty panel.

In Maryland, in the city where, in 1634, the ships the *Ark* and the *Dove* landed with the state's first settlers, St. Mary's College gives 1,500 fortunate students a good college experience in a water resort setting, at a third of the cost of a private college. But with out-of-state enrollment at only 15 percent, the weekend exodus is heavy. After the first edition of this book called it one of the rare public academic bargains, applications soared.

For countless New Yorkers and others with good grades who don't want to or can't get into an Ivy League school, that state offers in Harpur College, the liberal arts component of the State University at Binghamton, something as good or better. In most other states, a low-cost public institution of such high quality for the undergraduate would make the competition tough for the good private colleges. But since New York and New England didn't even make a start toward providing public higher education until the middle of the twentieth century, the natives have tended to think of anything public as second-rate—an attitude that would be incomprehensible to college-seekers in California, Michigan, North Carolina, Virginia, or Wisconsin, for example.

Binghamton has always been the unit in the state system committed to the liberal arts, although it has schools of nursing, management, engineering, and professional education.

And although it has three thousand graduate as well as ninety-five hundred undergraduate students, there is a strong commitment to teaching and to faculty-student contact, and its residential colleges have faculty masters as well as faculty fellows assigned to each. Until the early 1990s, fewer than 5 percent of Binghamton's students came from outside New York. Now, as the result of a program to increase diversity, the figure has climbed to 9 percent, and thirty-two states and forty-eight countries are represented.

Far larger, with about fourteen thousand students, Miami University in Oxford, Ohio, has few graduate assistants and less such teaching than any other public institution in the state, and as an undergraduate school it is head and shoulders above any of them. Its freshman class has a preschool orientation week in which the new students and teachers get acquainted, which contributes to a sense of community and personality. A beautiful campus and high standards have always made Miami an attractive alternative to an Ivy League school. And in recent years it has become nearly as selective as one for an out-of-stater.

Virginia has three public bargains: William and Mary, Mary Washington, and UVa at Wise. William and Mary, where Phi Beta Kappa was founded, is so selective that only very good students have a chance of getting in. And since the school can have only 30 percent out-of-state students, it is more selective than some of the Ivies for the non-Virginian, and nearly so for the natives, for whom, like the university in Charlottesville, it is a status symbol. The students are good, faculty members testify, but not venturesome or challenging; they reflect a conservative state. And the college does little to change them.

Mary Washington in Fredericksburg, a female satellite of the University of Virginia before the university went coed, is another former public bargain now selective. It accepts over half of its applicants, 80 percent of whom are Virginians, which means not much diversity, a heavy weekend exodus, and a comfortable, conventional atmosphere.

The third is UVa-Wise in southwestern Virginia, a school of 1,900 students with a goal of 2,000 (as of 2006) and the attractions of a good small college. Some students now go one year and transfer to the beautiful main campus at Charlottesville. If that should become a flood, it could endanger UVa-Wise's desirability. But the admissions director says a lot of the students planning this become attached and stay.

Minnesota has a good small campus at Morris, 160 miles northwest of Minneapolis, completely different from and far more desirable than the huge 46,000-student campus in the Twin Cities.

Alabama has Montevallo, about twice the size of Wise or Morris, but a small college compared to others in the state system.

Evergreen State College in Olympia, Washington, is an outstanding academic bargain, but it is as untraditional as Hampshire or St. John's or Deep Springs or New because it requires a commitment to learning that puts the monkey on the student's back. And most teenagers aren't ready for this. The first year, groups of sixty to one hundred students are team-taught by three to five faculty members in an interdisciplinary approach to a central theme. For more advanced work, a student may make an individual or a group contract for self-designed programs negotiated by faculty member and student. There are no grades, but rather faculty evaluations, and there are student evaluations of faculty as well. A clue to its ambience is that on a recent visit mine was the only jacket, or tie, anywhere on campus, whether dean, professor, or student. In this relaxed atmosphere there is a palpable sense of belonging.

A Lot of Colleges Are Church-related. Do They Indoctrinate?

Rarely is this a concern. While virtually every private college started life church-related, most such ties today are tenuous if they exist at all. Some few fundamentalist colleges, such as Liberty or Oral Roberts, have rigid rules of conduct and beliefs, or may, like Gordon College in Massachusetts, require that an applicant declare Christ as his savior, but they are the exceptions. The Methodist and Presbyterian colleges that a few decades ago had curfews for women—and some even for men—now have coed dorms and may sell beer in the student unions. Catholic colleges still require religion courses but may have Jews and Protestants in the theology departments. Academically, a wind has been blowing through the Catholic colleges, but they still tend to be homogeneous. Georgetown, a "hot" college, has 40 percent non-Catholic students, but most of the other big-name Catholic schools, like Notre Dame, Boston College, Holy Cross, or Villanova, are more homogeneous, with 80 to 90 percent Catholics. A student at Holy Cross, trying to sum it up for a *Time* reporter, said, "We're all white Anglo-Saxon Protestants here."

What Good Are Liberal Arts Colleges for My Career Needs?

Until the shifting sands of a developing service economy re-vived interest in them, parents and students too often per-ceived the "liberal arts" as vague, unfocused, pointing to no career, and therefore impractical. Too many still do, and the next time the job market gets discouraging, parents again will want their college students to have specific job goals in mind, no matter what the evidence that that's not the payoff. If, after four expensive years of college, stories of Joe and Jane waiting tables or driving a cab with no idea of what they want to do are on every neighbor's clucking tongue, parents will feel they have a social disease. And rising college costs will aggravate their condition. They will want a college that has a menu of suitable vocational programs—advertising, business, law, or whatever—that they envision as being hooked securely into the market for a first job.

In most cases, they could not be more wrong, for two rea-sons. The first, a reflection of the swiftness of change in our economy, is an upheaval in the ways people earn their living. Most of the fast-growing list of careers in the occupational directories, like most of the wonder drugs on the pharma-cists' shelves, weren't there before World War II, which means the manpower experts have been pretty good prophets. They have been saying for years that because of the changing nature of and the fast-growing list of kinds of work, today's students are likely to have three or four different careers or branches off a main stem. And what's more, a lot of those careers have yet to come into existence.

It follows that the supposed security of a now profitable role in the American establishment is about gone. Increasingly, new opportunities are springing up that only the prepared brain can envision and exploit. That wonderful quality of serendipity, often mistaken for luck, opens to the enlightened person new ways to use her talents and interests in satisfying pursuits. The specialist, wearing the blinders of her training, may be unable to envision and exploit new opportunities. She is the more likely candidate for what Thoreau called a life of quiet desperation.

The second reason parents are wrong is that people, as well as their options, change and grow. Hardly anyone has a crystal ball clear enough to divine what's going to appeal to her fifteen years hence. And the parents are themselves walking proofs that their worry about their son or daughter getting that first job is groundless. Just as their adult successes screen from their memories their own teenage uncertainties and shortcomings, so they cannot understand why their eighteen-year-olds don't know what they want to do and get about the business of doing it. But the kids are not failures, and the parents need not be ashamed; it's a normal situation. The parents were probably in the same boat a generation earlier.

To test that belief, when the job market became discouraging in the late 1970s, I started asking an additional biographical question of all the fathers and mothers who came to my office; namely, what their original college majors had been as freshmen. I knew what the answers would be. In 1970, the Carnegie Corporation had funded a study to find out whether a college major was a reliable indicator of a person's future vocation. It was not.

In only three fields—engineering, teacher education, and business administration—did the majority remain true to their choices. Fifteen years out of college, 75 to 96 percent of the men in all the other fields, whether the humanities, arts, social sciences, sciences, or mathematics, had forsaken their original interests. Women proved even more changeable. And there are some important caveats to come on those fields where people have tended to stay.

What I've found has been strikingly similar. Of over three thousand individuals, fewer than 10 percent have stayed in the fields which they originally chose as majors. Most are in careers not even remotely related. The bulk of the faithful are women who had planned to be teachers, because for many years a teaching certificate guaranteed a job.

Not only have nine out of ten of these parents changed careers, but many have made two or three changes. One father who had majored in economics in preparation for taking over the family furniture business tired of that and finally yielded to a long-held urge to have his own kennel. He was happy in that until a psychologist friend took him along on a visit to a state institution. The next day he telephoned to ask if he could go back to school and get a master of social work degree, the experience had so fired him up. He did, and he now has an additional role: social worker.

Another father shifted from psychology to owning a group of car washes and selling equipment for them, and still another moved from an engineering degree to one in law and a career in the Justice Department. Another apostate engineer became an administrative law judge. A mother who was a fine arts major now heads special education for a block of suburban schools.

A successful industrial realty developer had first tried chemistry and then social relations at Harvard. A management consultant got as far as a master's degree in physics before finding his true love. A fledgling geologist who is a corporate official was a presidential environment adviser.

The owner of a popular Baltimore restaurant is a registered pharmacist, while the head of a coffee-shop chain there is a German literature major. Another German lit major shifted in graduate school to political science and economics and became a Central Intelligence Agency economist. A Washington investment firm and an insurance brokerage firm are owned, respectively, by the holder of a master's degree in geography and a science major.

A Hopkins faculty member's doctorate in political science was a jump from his original major, business, while a former political scientist now runs a travel agency in Baltimore.

English literature majors are scattered all over the employment scene twenty years out of college and in roles worlds removed from their major. One is a budget official at the National Institutes of Health; another switched to anthropology and directs a study of metropolitan problems for this same agency of many concerns. A third was director of several major programs in what was the Department of Health, Education and Welfare. A high official of the Organization of American States thought philosophy was his field until he fell for law and then for international relations.

The parents who are still doing something stemming from their undergraduate interests tend to be doctors (but some were music, art history, and sociology majors), accountants, college faculty members, schoolteachers, businessmen, and engineers. And many of the last are no longer in engineering; they're in management, dealing with people. One of the faithful few, however, a successful builder and developer, says of his business administration major at Rutgers, "It was absolutely useless!"

And some of those who never complete a major also find happiness, like a CIA official who says he was tossed out of a most prestigious school.

It's hardly surprising then that studies consistently show that:

- Two-thirds of the college students change their career plans at least once, often twice, in those four years, and in a new economy, the number is rising.
- Most graduates change jobs at least once in the first five years after college, even on the graduate level. Harvard found it happens even to its master of business administration alumni.
- Only 30 percent of those who start in engineering graduate, chiefly because it does demand an early commitment.
- Two-thirds of the administrators in business did not major in that field.

Because no one knows how the fabric of his or her life will be woven and thus what may turn out to be relevant, learning is negative as well as positive. It may be just as important to discover after a semester or a year on the wrong track that one doesn't really like engineering or psychology as it is to find that one's real love is art history or economics. The chemists say that nothing ever ceases to exist. In education it is hard to think of any experience that is wasted—even a dead end—if it helps a person find out who he is.

The knowledge may come in handy in some wholly unexpected way. A young woman who graduated from Michigan with a degree in biology said that on cap and gown day she asked herself, "Why did I do this? I don't want to teach, and I'm not interested in being a research scientist." So she went back and got a master of administration degree. The combination qualified her for what was then a new kind of job: figuring out, in the Environmental Protection Agency, the environmental impact of a proposed commercial or industrial installation.

The Best Plan: Prepare to Cope

A teenager planning for college and a parent thinking of how he's going to pay for it often can't see why a liberal education is a better investment than a specialized one because the return as measured by first-job prospects seems too chancy. Like the Federal Reserve Board's tightening or loosening of the money supply, the effects of a real education take a while to show up. The liberal arts graduate quite often has more trouble finding his first job than does the engineer, accountant, or other specialist. But he winds up better satisfied and—because he has learned to think, to adapt, and to communicate—eventually may be the specialist's boss. Making decisions aimed at a first job is like assuming the first-inning score is going to be the final one. That kind of thinking can damage people's lives.

If You Feel Committed to a Big School

Be as choosy as you can. Try to get into an honors program for the top students, or get into a residential college, or any other select small-group program that seems suitable to you. Even if you don't meet the required grade point average, it may be possible to petition to get into individual honors classes. They have the better teachers, better, more involved students, and smaller classes. They are more demanding and, as a consequence, more stimulating. And besides doing you more good, they are likely to impress a prospective employer. The residential or other small-group programs will give a sense of community within the big university and perhaps a lot more contact with professors than the general school population has.

So What Is the Message?

The message is that a good selecting job deserves as much research and hard thinking as a term paper, and will do more for you.

Assuming that you have done the self-examination and have an idea of why you're going and what you want, you must then read, read, read, and use the Internet. There's no getting away from this. Here are some things to keep in mind:

1. Settle on your priorities and hold to them.

Don't get mired in irrelevancies. Don't worry about the proximity of ski slopes or beaches or geography or climate.

Don't fall victim to the instant-gratification impulse. The fun items will be plentiful enough. Besides, there'll be plenty of playtime on campus, not to mention off-campus study programs in this country and abroad. College is no convent; indeed, the trouble is not too few temptations but too many.

2. Reread chapter 1, "Twenty-one Myths."

Doing this may help keep you on track if you think, like so many high school seniors, that you need to be in or near a city, or that your college must have an enrollment of "at least five thousand," as so many (usually girls) specify. Or you may think there's some magic in geography, or that you're afraid your friends—whom you probably won't even know five years hence—may not have heard of it.

These considerations are the nearly universal irrelevancies I've tried to disabuse clients of. And if many of them who went to colleges that were (a) not near a city, (b) much smaller than five thousand, and (c) had little name recognition had been dissatisfied, I would soon have been in some other line of work.

Doing that reading and using the Internet may reassure you of good company, plenty of competition, and as lively a life outside class as you want. And if it leads you to consider schools you otherwise wouldn't have, it may prove a good lifetime investment.

3. Don't rule out a college because you don't like that state.

For example, at the mention of West Virginia, parents' eyes often glaze over. One year it happened with four families. All four visited the colleges discussed, and all four students went. One of the fathers on his return called to say, "West Virginia Wesleyan is a fabulous place!" Similarly, a mother who had been apprehensive about Kansas jubilantly reported, "Kansas City is a wonderful place!" What's more, her son got good enough grades at Park College to get into medical school, something he couldn't have done at the University of Maryland.

A well-to-do Baltimore mother whose reservations about Davis and Elkins were geographical wrote four years later to say how much that college had done for her son's personal and mental development.

Once, after I'd suggested some midwestern colleges for a bright girl with middling grades, her Harvard College, Harvard Law father demanded, "Why are all those schools in Iowa?" "Because," I answered, "they're better than the selective ones in the East she can't get into."

4. Cast off home-state shackles in reaching your decision.

This can be just as important as letting a geographical prejudice rule out a college. A lot of people who otherwise use their noggins think they can and will come home more often if they go to a college in-state because it will be handier. I asked a girl who'd gone to a college in southwest Virginia for this reason how many times she'd come home to Alexandria—other than holidays—in four years. "None," she said. And if she had, a lot of closer places in other states, or farther away but handier to airports, would have made for easier traveling. All she had done was to narrow her options. Besides, if a program is sufficiently demanding, it's going to require some time in the library most weekends. And with so many on-campus activities, why would you want to leave?

5. Don't feel limited by finances to the nearest or cheapest place.

If the family income is that low, you will qualify for financial aid, and it literally may be cheaper to go away to an expensive private college than live at home and go to a free public one. More than one financial aid officer has said too many parents just assume they're not eligible for aid and don't ask. Some states, however, do give aid grants for use only in that state.

6. Don't be blinded by offers of an athletic scholarship.

If the Federal Trade Commission ever started prosecuting the frauds in this area, there'd be a lot of presidents as well as coaches under indictment. (Clemson's president resigned when the board of trustees refused to let him clean up things there, which gives a clue to the lack of a Clemson ethos.) The scholarship may be revoked if you don't make the team or if you get hurt. And as Dr. Jan Kemp, who was fired by the University of Georgia for fighting for an honest athletic tutoring program, sued, and won back her job and a $1 million damage award, said, "It's still the plantation system, but the slaves are scoring touchdowns instead of picking cotton, and if they don't produce, they can't live in the big house."

But more important, this is making a central decision for the wrong reason. One of my young friends, who had decided the Great Books program at St. John's College was just the thing for him, went to the University of Virginia when offered a track scholarship. He stayed one semester and transferred to St. John's. He'd gotten his priorities back in order.

The Other Side of the Coin: Things to Do

1. Step your choices down; don't make them all at one level, or top and bottom.

Too many people make the mistake of trying for two or three at the top of their lists and then dropping way down in quality or desirability to schools that are clearly safe, only because they are safe. In so doing, they sacrifice quality and some of the good they should get from college. If they had taken the trouble to find out about more colleges—ones they'd never heard of—they'd have profited happily. And the colleges they didn't know about before might prove better than their original choices.

2. Pick a school because you like its ethos, its atmosphere, what it stands for, because it fits you, not because you've heard it has a good department in the subject you plan to major in. You may well change your major two or three times; most people do.

If it's an undergraduate college, almost any department is going to offer a lot more than you're going to be able to take away in four years. Teenagers are misled by this quality-of-department talk. Faculty PhDs are journeymen who've attained the doctoral level by negotiating the same rigorous course, and in this age of a soft academic market, any college that doesn't have qualified faculty hasn't tried, or has a lot of tenured faculty who can't be fired.

The important thing is whether they are good teachers whose primary interest is in teaching and students rather than research. The famous scholar in the university may not give undergraduates the time of day.

Remember, too, that the professor who has gotten to know you can write a far more cogent and persuasive recommendation than the one to whom you may be a face in the lecture hall, if that.

3. Pick the college that looks like it will be the most demanding one you can get into.

This may not be the most selective one; indeed, you may be surprised at how much harder you'll have to work at some college that accepts most of its applicants than at some very selective ones. The college that does something for you is the one that challenges you; otherwise, you're wasting your time.

4. Use the directories to get some indicators, such as the percentage that goes on to graduate study in what fields, what percentage leaves campus on weekends, what the most popular majors are, and whether it's residential or commuter, a no-no.

5. Use the telephone, Internet, or e-mail to ask admissions and faculty people questions about how much time students spend studying, how many pages they read a night, or whatever else may concern you. Consult the catalogs for faculty and staff names. The librarian is a good one to try to ask for help. Most faculty members will level with you. Call or e-mail the student newspaper or any student organizations you can locate. This is worth the effort and can lead to a visit or supplement one.

Alumni in your area are a good source of information; in fact, one of them may interview you if you apply. Now is a good time to get in the first lick and make her be the subject. The school will probably give you the names of nearby alums who are willing to talk to students.

6. Don't consider commuter schools; they're not likely to have any sense of community or to provide the close relationship with teachers, the collaborative learning, the emphasis on values, or the other important qualities of the good small college.

7. Avoid schools that are heavily preprofessional or devoted to teacher education. You need a liberal education now; you can specialize later. A good college will give you not only an education but also the courses needed for certification. If you want to be an engineer, consider starting at a liberal arts college and taking the 3–2 route (three years at a liberal arts college and two at an engineering school). If you must go to an engineering school, find out how much liberal arts is required. This is important because a few years out of college you may be an administrator, which calls for abilities such as people skills that engineering courses don't develop.

Pick the least vocationally oriented program you can. After the freshman year at least, there's likely to be more contact with teachers, smaller classes, more learning, and less training. Also, you will learn more philosophy from a first-rate teacher in economics than a second-rate one in philosophy, so look for the best teachers and the toughest ones, not the popular, easy-grading lecturers. The good ones are those who have high expectations of their students as well as of themselves. On every faculty in the land, there are clunks and there are people who can make a difference in your life. Seek them out.

Remember that as important as selecting the right college is, the attitude with which you go is even more important. Indeed, attitude is 95 percent of the battle, in college or anywhere else.

CHAPTER 9

There Are New Ground Rules on What College Can Do

SOCIETY USUALLY ISN'T AWARE IT'S suffering from cultural lag because change comes in gradually, without fanfare. But it does give clues along the way. One such was a 1982 story in *Engineering News* that the 1957 Yale class at its twenty-fifth reunion found that three-quarters of that elite group were working at jobs that hadn't existed when they were in school. Another was the award of the 1987 Nobel Prize for economics to Dr. Robert Solow, who demonstrated that growth was not coming from the old gospel: increases in capital or machinery. Rather, he said, growth comes from increases in knowledge and the resulting advances in technology and human skills and understanding.

But, like generals fighting the last war, people think the prestige college is the one that guarantees the good life.

It is not. What ensures the good life is the small college that transforms an individual into an effective adult with powers she didn't know she had. Such a college is concerned with the kind of person a student becomes, not whom she gets to know during those four years.

Ours has become a knowledge society, which means constant change—ever more new jobs and careers, with no old-boy networks. Furthermore, the rate of change will only quicken, because there is so much more brainpower at work than ever before. Mathematics is the basic tool that makes possible advances in the other sciences: space travel and the supercomputer, for example. And as is true for mathematicians, about 97 percent of all the scientists who've ever lived are alive today, a critical mass.

Back in the 1990s, the Bureau of Labor Statistics predicted that nine out of ten jobs would soon be in the managerial, the professional, and the technical fields, to be filled by college graduates. That forecast was right on the mark; college graduates get the jobs while the Rust Belt reflects shrinking industrial profits and the diminishing clout of the unions.

Furthermore, Samuel Ehrenhalt, a bureau official, predicted at the same time that the rewards in the new economy would depend on creativity, independent thought and action, and, above all, on ideas and the ability to exploit the new knowledge. He did not mention connections or school prestige. Unknowingly, he was listing qualities that the good college experience develops.

The upheavals of a new kind of economy have also shifted wealth and power from the Establishment Northeast to the Noveau Riche Southwest. It is bypassing old arrangements in favor of the prepared and alert individual. So does the gold rush of college graduates to seek their fortunes in dozens of countries that have become potential mother lodes. In Russia or a dozen other countries, the name of your college would probably draw a blank stare.

In short, the old order is gone. The evidence is overwhelming. The vast corporate downsizing of the early 1990s, as detailed in chapter 1, proved for good that an Ivy degree doesn't guarantee career success. Of the top fifty CEOs of the Fortune 500 companies, only seven are Ivy graduates. America's scientists and scholars come disproportionately from the good small colleges rather than from the Ivies or other research universities.

What makes such facts so telling is that the prestige institutions pick the country's ablest students. They skim off only a small percentage of the top high school achievers, even of the valedictorians. All this says four things: first, the prestige schools are doing such a lousy job that they confirm the exposé of Dr. Stanley Katz that liberal education in the research universities is "in ruins." Second, prestige doesn't account for much. Third, academic aptitude is a minor matter in life. And fourth, the good small college produces growth.

Ethics, a main concern of the good small college, are not a minor matter. An article in the *Economist* points out that Enron, Arthur Andersen, and Long Term Capital Management all had been using consultants to load up on talent and skill. They hired 250 MBAs a year, but they overlooked the secret ingredient, morals. As in Shakespeare's *Henry V*, "for want of a nail a shoe was lost. For want of a shoe a horse was lost." And the firms succumbed to greed and mismanagement. Their fate was "terrifyingly sudden."

The article also predicts a good market for the educated person: America's biggest 500 companies will lose half their senior managers by 2010 or thereabouts, and the next generation of potential leaders has already been decimated by the reengineering and downsizing of the past few decades. At the top of the civil service, the attrition rate will be even higher.

At the same time, employees will be in the driver's seat. Thanks to all that downsizing, the old social contract—job security in return for commitment—has been breaking down, and most people now don't hesitate to take other jobs.

In the past, technical breakthroughs such as the plow, the printing press, the steam engine, and the landmark inventions of the eighteenth and early nineteenth centuries were the work of ingenious tinkerers and enterprisers. Things began to change in the nineteenth century, but even so, fifty years elapsed between the discovery of the electric generator in 1830 and electric lights. The gap between Einstein's theory of relativity and the atomic bomb was forty years; between the discovery of the master molecule of life, DNA, and commercial genetic engineering, twenty years. But it was only six years between the 1957 discovery of the electron's abilities and the commercial production of electrical diodes for transistor radios and computers.

In short, scientific discovery and a resulting technology now almost go hand in glove. Some American patents cite fifty or more scientific papers, twice as many as in Japan and far ahead of Britain, France, or Germany. It is because America leads the world in basic research and development that the gap between a scientific paper and a commercial patent has shrunk in this country to six years.

Every study, every indicator, says the wise thing is to go to a place and take courses with teachers that may bring out your special qualities. When men and women in midlife are asked to look back on their college experiences, in overwhelming numbers they say that what they remember are the values, the standards, the stimulus to continue developing themselves. Most of the course content has been forgotten.

Employers of all kinds—state, federal, and private—have confirmed what the old grads say. When the job market was bad in the late 1970s, several liberal arts colleges got federal or foundation grants to find out what would make their graduates attractive to employers. What they found was that employers uniformly were much more interested in the applicant's ability to think and to communicate, as revealed by her ability to write a coherent paragraph or résumé or to conduct a sensible, grammatical interview, than in her major, her grades, or the name of her college. Equally important were the human qualities, the ability to obtain the cooperation and the respect of others. Indeed, one faculty team wrote that they were "astonished to discover" that these things were more important than the applicant's academic background, the reputation of the college or university, personal connections, or even grades.

This discovery of a new set of ground rules in the job market echoed in part those of a Haverford psychology professor, Dr. Douglas Heath, who for forty years studied the effects of that rigorous Quaker college on its graduates. It is a surpassingly successful group, and the principal influence on their development has been their undergraduate college. And the outstanding quality of these men (the first class of women graduated in 1985), as rated by their professional colleagues, has been their ethical integrity.

For many years the word *moral* has been shunned by students as well as faculty, even though all the crucial decisions of life are subjective value judgments, not cool cerebrations of pure, trained reason.

The alumni of Haverford—like those of many other good colleges—have long been testifying that *moral* is the central word, and that the good small college is the one most likely to be the blinding light on the road to Damascus.

This group provides unusually good evidence: over 80 percent of them have advanced degrees, whether in medicine, law, business management, engineering, social work, or one of the academic disciplines. Over 20 percent of them have taught in major colleges and universities. Over 40 percent have secured patents or published books, articles, or poems, and many have received postcollege awards. Several were presidents or managers of their firms.

The Haverford alumni said their graduate or professional schools did little or nothing to help them develop the qualities of character that contributed to their success. Only one lawyer spoke of a course in law school that examined ethical values. And, Dr. Heath noted, "Although the majority of them were being educated to serve others, only one said his professional school reinforced his desire to serve them."

Dr. Heath's findings hit him hard enough to make him change his whole mode and emphasis in teaching his own courses at Haverford. His research also confirms what Philip Jacob of the University of Pennsylvania reported several decades ago in *Changing Values in College*. Dr. Jacob said that teachers and institutions that set high standards for themselves, that critically examine their own values and expect the same from their students, do influence their intellectual and moral development. However, relatively few teachers or institutions do this.

Indeed, Dr. Heath said that at his own alma mater (Amherst), "I was seldom challenged by the faculty or the college's ethos to confront self-consciously my own values; I received an excellent intellectual education but I was not much affected by the college." An education that "does not work itself into a man's values, challenge his view of himself, and alter his relations with others, is unlikely to produce many nurturing effects that persist," he added. Years later, a college president told me her daughter "had a good time but wasn't changed" by Amherst.

The years 1988 and 1989 might be considered notable for two reasons: one, the government started taking official notice of the greenhouse effect of atmospheric pollution on the planet; and two, there was an increased awareness of *moral* values. For the first time since Woodrow Wilson's address in 1902, a new Princeton president, Harold Shapiro, dealt with moral values in his installation address. Giving students the ability and desire to engage in the moral discourse required to give meaning to our national life, he asserted, was the university's most important job. But most universities fail to do this. As sociologist Robert Bellah and other researchers have concluded, with a few exceptions the university is a place where one goes to fulfill private dreams of individual success. It does not develop these moral values.

If there were any research like Heath's to discover whether name or prestige contributes as much to success as a school's ethos, the findings undoubtedly would be startling. A lot of little-known colleges would be found to equal or outperform many well-known ones. Many schools that are barely or not at all selective consistently outperform some of our top research universities in the production of scholars and scientists.

As Dr. Heath says, it is the quality of the experience, not its name, that is the key.

Especially in a swiftly changing, growing economy, the personal qualities the college has developed are the critical factors. Four years of college can't make anyone a practitioner in any field that isn't routine or formulaic, and as all alumni can testify, when surveyed, the course content has evaporated anyway. Today, more than ever, no one has a crystal ball clear enough to see the career landscape even ten years hence. Dental schools are closing. Teaching certificates once were gilt-edged. Other popular fields may become overcrowded or even obsolete. Engineering has its swings from feast to famine, and when it's famine, these specialists can't adapt to a changing job market as easily as the generalists who have developed the mental agility to adapt. Furthermore, engineers—like other specialists—need nonspecialist savvy as they move up, like dealing with people.

AT&T, before its breakup, did a self-study that went further. That giant technical corporation dominated by engineers wanted to find out if a liberal arts graduate could survive there. He did, and very well, thank you. While only 10 percent of AT&T's employees had liberal arts degrees, 43 percent of them achieved at least the fourth level of management—a measure of considerable success. Only 23 percent of the engineers did as well.

The AT&T spokesman said,

> We discovered that in the managing of a business the liberal arts people were not wedded to a particular idea or approach; they were open; they were more creative. A linear manager [translate: engineer] would try to fit a problem into a specific box. The engineer felt comfortable with a small group of likes, but when he expanded his scope, his comfort dropped. The nonlinear executive did a better job of communicating; the engineer was more militaristic; the nonlinear executive was more receptive.
>
> The future is to the creative, the leap-taker. An engineering company is no longer limited to engineers. It is influenced by what happens today in Korea or Königsberg. It is very different from the old days.

The familial college that compels the youth to do the kind of internal and external exploration that affects the development of values and sharpens and enlightens the mind is the one most likely to develop the creative, the leap-taker for the future. And whatever its name, or whether you've ever heard of it, that kind of college will pay the richest lifelong dividends.

An Important Feminist Note

In a university administrative group meeting in the 1960s to discuss scholarship policies, the chancellor suggested giving them only to men because the women would just get married and have families. "Like Mrs. Compton," I said, "whose three sons were presidents of MIT, the University of Washington, and Washington University, and one of whom was a Nobel Prize winner, not to mention a lawyer daughter distinguished enough to get an honorary doctorate of laws." The suggestion was dropped.

That attitude may no longer be prevalent, but the incident illustrates one of the reasons I've always believed the education of a girl to be more important than that of a boy. Her planning should be less influenced by current fashion; it should be at least as long-range and basic as that of her brother because her life is likely to involve more variables than his. Her education should make her versatile, give her room for growth and future maneuver. Why?

First, because the probabilities today are greater than ever that she will start a career, interrupt it for several months to several years while she has a child or is at home with children, maybe even until they're in high school, and then go back to work. While she's out, both the job market and her interests may change. It seems to me that not only are nearly all of the well-off mothers I talk to working outside the home, but also that they are doing things they would never have guessed they'd be doing when they were in college.

The Census Bureau supports me in this. It has now certified that the working mother has become a way of life. In 1987, for the first time, more than half of the nation's new mothers remained in the job market or returned within a year. For mothers with college degrees the figure was 63 percent. The bureau did not offer any figures on what percentage returned after several years, but noted that two-thirds of the widowed, divorced, or separated mothers were working.

It also said that in more than 40 percent of all families with parents in the childbearing ages of eighteen to forty-four, both parents worked.

The second and more important reason is that, like Mrs. Compton, the mother is the source of comfort, the day-long standard-setter, and the principal influence on the character and the aspirations of the next generation. Q.E.D.

CHAPTER 10

What Are You Going For, Really?

IN A MAJOR STUDY IN the mid-1980s, a panel of academicians reported that many students had only vague notions of what an undergraduate education is all about or where it is supposed to lead. One of several reasons is that most teenagers have not spent much, if any, time asking themselves exactly why they want to go to college. Years ago, a client who was a top student, debater, editor, and athlete said in the course of talking about college choices, "Well, it's four years out of my life, anyway." As a senior at Stanford he admitted, "I am a bit aghast that I said those words."

Another reason, as the academicians would have known if they'd gone to small colleges, is that most adolescents don't yet know who they are or what they want to do with their lives. College is partly a search for those things, both in and out of class.

Still another is the fog surrounding the search, according to nearly half of the five thousand college students quizzed for *College: The Undergraduate Experience in America*, the most comprehensive survey yet made of U.S. colleges and universities, headed by Ernest L. Boyer of the Carnegie Foundation for the Advancement of Teaching. There was often no sound basis for making a decision, Boyer's team concluded. One reason is our woeful lack of consumer research on our colleges and universities. The other is that few teenagers confront the question at all. Doing that also requires a readiness to recognize what's there. That may take a little work, but it's worth it, since what happens in college powerfully affects the quality of a person's life.

Most adolescents obviously expend more effort on learning how to water-ski or earning a driver's license than on making an informed college choice. Otherwise it wouldn't be the case that each year over 2.5 million freshmen enter college, but only about 975,000 seniors graduate. That's a production rate of a little better than one-third. Furthermore, of those who do stay, many persist unhappily to graduation, unaffected and disaffected, unaware of what they've missed. Credentials are all they have to show for a barren marriage.

The first order of business in making a profitable college investment is to heed the injunction "Know thyself." And that's what this chapter is about. Hence it is addressed primarily to the student (the next chapter is for parents' reassurance). Any intelligent parent already knows what I'm going to say and would tell the teenager the same things, if only he didn't suffer the communication handicap of being a parent. Parents should still try to get the idea across, but not too hard; overkill is an occupational hazard of parenthood.

It takes both clarity and courage to look at yourself probingly and then make decisions based on what you see there, rather than being influenced by friends or classmates. In more than thirty-five years of talking to high school juniors and seniors, I have learned that many of them lack any clear idea of what kind of lives they want to lead. They are taken by surprise when I ask them what their abilities, strengths, and weaknesses are, what their goals in life are, and what they would say if they had to decide right now how they would like to spend the working hours of their lives for the next ten years, if they could not change in that time. And these are children of affluent professional, often prominent, parents.

If the student doesn't look to himself, he's vulnerable to herd thinking, one of the principal causes of bad decisions. For example, when five hundred seniors in a class of five hundred at Churchill High School, in a Maryland suburb of Washington, D.C., apply to Indiana University and ignore such first-rate places in that state as Earlham, Wabash, De-Pauw, and Notre Dame, that shows appalling evidence of a sheep mentality at work in which a lot of adolescents are making blind and probably wrong decisions. Similarly, when sixty-five in a class of four hundred mostly able students at nearby Walter Johnson High make the mass-production state university or one of its provincial satellites their choice, and another fifty apply to like universities out of state, a lot of good kids are shortchanging themselves—permanently.

This happens all over the country. A valedictorian in Memphis's best high school was regarded as a traitor of sorts because she broke ranks and chose Ohio Wesleyan over the University of Tennessee. Nor could friends or teachers in Seattle understand why a promising boy wanted to go away from Washington.

The student must do his homework. Neither his parents, his peers, his high school teachers, nor his counselors can do it for him. Indeed, the more he lets others into the process, the greater the risk of botching the job. The worst risk is listening to one's peers. They are the most dismally ignorant of all sources of guidance except for a university athletic recruiter.

What do one's high school peers know about colleges? Next to nothing. They know the names of name schools, and that's about it. And while most teachers and counselors "know about" fifteen or twenty colleges, they know little or nothing about these colleges' virtues, faults, or other differences among them. That kind of expertise takes on-the-spot research that high school staff have never had either the money or the time for. Furthermore, many teachers and counselors went to teacher-education institutions, and a rigorous liberal arts education may not be in their experience. Even more to the point, they don't know enough about a student to know how the various schools' virtues or faults would affect him. He is the one who has to know himself if he is to make a wise decision.

The homework I'm suggesting can't be completed in one session or one day if the student has never seriously looked into himself. But try it today and let it simmer, think about it; then try it again next week.

The first thing to do is ask a silly question:

Why Am I Going in the First Place?

Is it because I wouldn't dare not go; I'd be an outcast if I didn't? Is it because I think it will lead to a good job, because I want to be a doctor or a lawyer or a corporate executive, because I want the social life, good skiing, football weekends, a big city, the bragging rights of a prestige college, or an intellectual challenge and a place that will help me grow?

A great deal hangs on how searchingly that question is asked and how candidly it is answered.

What Do I Want Most Out of College? Least?

This also requires some hard thinking. Is skiing a top priority, or having a city nearby? Does an athletic scholarship outweigh the advantages that might be evident long after the athletic career?

What About the Trade-offs?

Would I rather go to Penn because it's Ivy, it's big and in a city, and I think it might be an easier entrée to a job, or go to Haverford or Kenyon because in the small college I'd be involved in my own education, and it might therefore be more stimulating and do more for me in the long run?

Should I pick a Villanova because it's in a city, or an Earlham because it's more demanding?

Do I need to be a big fish in a big pond, or do I need a more familiar atmosphere?

Those are questions to which there aren't any reliable answers until you decide on your priorities, not just for a four-year period but for the forty-year long term.

What Do I Want Out of Life, or in Life—Something Tangible or Intangible?

Do I want a comfortable space in the Establishment and a good country club membership, or to do my own thing? Do I want satisfaction or happiness, and what constitutes happiness?

Am I an acquisitor, a creator, a comforter, a venturer, or a problem solver?

Will I need to be involved with people or not?

Who am I? What are my abilities? What do I have to offer?

These priorities are also questions that a seventeen- or an eighteen-year-old may not be able to answer for himself with certainty, but thinking about them is a start, and perhaps some of the later chapters will help in deciding what kind of school may be better for the acquisitor and what kind for the venturer, and whether or not a particular school may pave the way.

Your Greatest Danger

Listening to your friends is not quite as bad as taking drugs, but it sure ruins a lot of college choices. Just say no. Be your own man or woman; it's your life. Every year I have at least a couple of clients who apply to Boston U, Syracuse, the University of Richmond, Indiana University, or some other place not nearly good enough for them simply because in their group those schools are all the rage. And every year I get other clients who went to unsuitable schools because they were the fashion and have flunked out or dropped out after a year or two and have to do the job all over again.

As Plato said, the unexamined life is not worth living. A crucial time to start making it worth living is in this period of deciding where to go. If others are the principal influence, it's blindman's bluff, and that's not the smart way.

And if the decision is to take a year off, that is sometimes the best thing. We'll examine the pros and cons of that in a later chapter.

CHAPTER 11

Sample and Test the Merchandise

When that Aprille with his shoures sote
The droghte of Marche hath perced to the rote,
And bathed every veyne in swich licour
Of which vertu engendered is the flour; . . .
Than longen folk to goon on pilgrimages
—THE CANTERBURY TALES, PROLOGUE

CHAUCER'S *CANTERBURY TALES* DEPICTED ONE of medieval England's great spring events, the salvation-seeking pilgrimages to the shrine of the martyred Saint Thomas à Becket. Were Chaucer alive today and chronicling America's spring and summer pilgrimages of college-seekers, he'd find them far more numerous, much more middle-class than motley, and the caravans tiny: usually two parents and a teenager or two. And rather than a common holy place, each little band would be seeking out three or four of its own: the campuses from which to pick the teenager's college of choice.

Should he choose to compare the efficacy of the medieval and the modern journeys, Chaucer would be compelled to give the nod to those who put their faith in the martyr. They at least lived thereafter in hope, whereas today's pilgrims often find their hopes turning to dross. This is partly because their pilgrimages are made at the wrong time, in the wrong way, and by the wrong folks. Also, they are looking at the physical trappings, possibly attending spring rites such as graduations that have little relevance to the quest, and more than likely missing the heart of the matter while assessing the real estate. This is one of many reasons why most college choices fail to last.

This chapter will tell you in detail how to be a smart pilgrim, and will list a lot of questions you should ask that will tell you whether a particular college would be a good choice for you.

In an ideal world of college-choosing, the pilgrim should go alone, on a school day, and spend a working day and a night doing a well-prepared, hard-nosed inquiry into the nature of the place and its inhabitants.

That should come after he has done these three things:

1. Read the catalog to see what the graduation requirements consist of, what special programs and off-campus experiences are offered, and whether there is any hint of what four years there might do for a student. This is important because in many places, especially many large public universities, it is not only possible but the easiest thing in the world to get a degree without ever getting anything faintly resembling an education. And that is what happens to most.

2. Complete a probing self-assessment, plus a draft or two of a personal statement, so you'll be better able to talk about yourself.

3. Make a list of questions to ask about what kinds of experiences others are having there. These should be things that are important to you, the pilgrim, however odd they might seem to someone else. And the questions may well change after the experience gained in the first visit. A sample list of questions will be given later on.

A parent may have objections to such a rigorous visiting procedure: "It takes a lot of work; my seventeen-year-old is too young to go alone, and besides, I want to go along." True, it is a lot of work, but very little compared to the importance of the project. The teenager won't be too young to go alone next fall; why is he now? The parents can and probably should go, but on condition they and the student part company at the campus gate. They can compare notes later. Going with a friend is a no-no for the same reason: the student may talk to the parents or friend instead of asking questions.

College costs somewhere between a Mercedes at a public institution and a Bentley at a private one, and it can have a profound influence on the quality of a person's life. So why choose one without inspecting the merchandise rather than its packaging, and without doing some comparison shopping?

A random example of what may happen otherwise—and it's one of the countless number of examples occurring at other institutions—is that of a suburban Washington boy and his father who had made only a summer visit to the University of Southern California the previous year. When they came to me, the father said, "Very clear representations were made to us that although this was a large university, classes were small, there was much personal contact, and plenty of individual counseling. What my son found was a mass-production mill of big classes, unavailable professors, easy courses, and rampant cheating." The son, who had made the dean's list, transferred to Claremont McKenna, a grade-A college with an enrollment of nine hundred, but only after doing the working-day investigation he should have done at USC. This effort really found for him the things the USC official had claimed.

Most colleges, but not often the universities, are happy to put visitors up overnight in the dorms and give them cafeteria passes. Some of the universities give group campus tours, which are of little value for probing the character of the place. A call to the admissions office will be sufficient to arrange a visit, and the person making the arrangements will probably ask what classes the visitor would like to attend, and whether an interview is desired.

Anxiety about interviews is great but vastly overblown. At few places and in few cases is it decisive or even very important, as chapter 15 will point out. What an applicant says in her written application and what the objective data on that record say about her are the critical elements. Besides, only a small fraction of applicants get to campuses for interviews.

If the number of school days available for visiting is much restricted, try traveling on a Sunday, going to classes

Monday, and getting back to high school for Tuesday classes. Or, travel Thursday afternoon, go to classes on Friday, and have the weekend to extend the visit if needed. The number of classes on Friday afternoon may be limited, however.

It is important to go as a customer, not as a supplicant. In that role, don't buy everything the college may tell you. They're all marketing their wares; their sales pitches may not cover the things that are important to you, and may need to be put in perspective or even taken with more than a grain of salt. Furthermore, even if you have done some self-examination, you may not fully realize at first look or hearing what things really will be important to you. It takes questioning to make the comparisons and the contrasts clear.

That means spending a day and a night, going to a few classes, eating in the cafeteria, and sleeping in the dorm. This gives you time to ask questions and to think of follow-ups, and the leisure to chat with students and faculty. Weekend visits aren't likely to produce anywhere near the same results as a visit on a working day.

Reactions to a visit may be as much visceral as cerebral, as are the major decisions of life, but the viscera will operate more truly if the brain is informed. Conclusions shouldn't be drawn on the basis of one or two opinions or on the impression made by the interviewer or the campus guide. For example, a good New England college alienated at least one girl's family because the student showing them around carried a can of beer, a sin he probably did not commit again. Or the campus tour guide may take the visitors past the library and into the student union and its video games, pinball machines, and snack bars. While a tour guide enthusiastic about the wrong things is at the very least a bad mark against the way the admissions office is run and should be taken seriously, it doesn't in itself necessarily disqualify the college.

Since in this rich country anyone can get into a college that can challenge him, whatever his academic abilities, the visitor should assume the role of probing consumer. There's no risk; there are so many good colleges of all kinds that if one school says no, at least one other will say yes. It may be beyond fantasy to expect a high school senior visiting Harvard or Stanford, for instance, to put on such confident armor but it is nonetheless true.

College-arranged visiting days for captive groups of prospects are what in pre-glasnost days were called Russian tours; they permit the college to put its best foot forward without permitting too-close scrutiny. Similarly, college nights and college fairs are circuses for selling the colleges. They do little or nothing to sort things out, even though the fair is full of sales managers.

Since every college visitor isn't looking for the same thing, the same questions won't work for everyone, but there are plenty of clues to whether a school is a good and comfortable fit. The important thing is to ask the questions that deal with your particular needs. The college may be right for a friend, or it may be the one that's popular in your high school. But maybe your friend likes vanilla, and you don't. Even less relevant is the college's popularity with other members of the senior class. The seniors at another school will, in their wisdom, be favoring a different college. At almost any suburban high school a large chunk of the class will apply to the same school, not because it offers a fine education but because it's peer-approved. Considering that the chances are at least a hundred to one that the paths and interests of high school friends will scatter them even in their first year of college, today's peer approval will turn out to be empty tomorrow, leaving some regrets.

To be a smart customer, make overnight visits to at least a couple of colleges if possible, for comparison's sake, and follow a plan like this:

Things to Do

1. Talk to a couple of dozen students and a few faculty members. This provides a better sample and can tell you whether a bad impression is a fluke or characteristic. The praise or the gripe that is out of the pattern can be put in perspective, and you're in less danger of kissing off a good place or buying a pig in a poke. Don't spend your time with just one or two people.

2. Go to at least two classes. A typical freshman class, especially if it's a required general education course, and perhaps an upper-division class in your area of interest, are useful choices.

3. Eat in the cafeteria. That's the place where you'll get more answers to more questions than almost anywhere else. And sit at a big table where six to eight kids are sitting; that way you'll get a lot of responses to your questions.

4. Visit the faculty offices; knock on some doors and ask questions. This is where you'll get a slant on the students and answers you might not get anywhere else.

5. Visit the bookstore. Fifteen minutes here will tell you a lot about the character of the school. If it has virtually all textbooks, with little or nothing for secondary reading or independent study and no general literature, but lots of beer mugs, ashtrays, glasses, and pennants with the college seal, it may indicate a lot of college spirit but not much intellectual orientation. Inexpensive classical music and art prints and a wide range of good books, on the other hand, are a very good sign.

6. Visit the newspaper and, if there is one, the radio station. Here are people who ought to have their fingers on the pulse of the place.

7. Visit the student government office for the same reason.

8. Investigate the library and its use.

9. Have an admissions interview if the college wants it, or if you have questions you want to ask, such as, would I be accepted?

10. Spend a night in the dorm. This means a longer, less hurried visit and a chance to think about what you've learned and whether you need to ask some follow-up questions in the morning.

Questions to Ask of Students and of Yourself

■ What are the chief gripes of people around here? This is a good opener that gets things going. When I asked a former client, a sophomore, his response was, "It's awfully hard to be humble at Amherst." But usually this question gives some revealing clues and suggestions for further diggings. For example, if they say it's hard to get the classes you want or that the professors are distant, those are alarm bells. On the other hand, if they want you to know that they've found the way, the truth, and the life, that's great, but make sure that it is also for you. At St. John's College, where there are Great Books and no electives, I asked a couple of girls who'd transferred from the University of California at Berkeley if it bothered them that they couldn't have a course in psychology under someone like Eric Erikson at Harvard. The comeback was, "Oh, no. We can go to the library and read all that." But the regimen that has been described as four years discussing what is truth is not for everybody.

■ Are most classes lectures, with everyone madly taking notes to regurgitate on the next exam, or are they discussions? A great deal more work is required of both teacher and student in a discussion class. The teacher must have questions to cover every point he would make in a lecture. (As a professor acquaintance said at a 2:00 a.m. breakup of a poker game, "Well, I'm not prepared; I'll have to lecture today.") The student has to be prepared because he's expected to be a participant in the discussion class, not a passive ear.

■ Do the students take an active part in the discussion, or is the class lifeless? Don't depend on your observation of one or two classes for the answer to this; ask several students.

■ Do the professors give essay or multiple-choice exams? The latter are easy-to-grade cop-outs. Many students at top state universities like Berkeley and even at popular private places like Vanderbilt don't write a paper of any kind in four years. This is inexcusable, and it's cheating you!

■ After class, do any students hang around to ask questions or continue the discussion, or does everyone clear out pronto?

■ Is there any discussion about what went on in class?

■ Do students stay around after meals, arguing about ideas? Or is the conversation about the weekend?

■ What are the principal reasons students leave or transfer out? This is well worth asking even if the registrar or friend may not have gotten any reason for leaving, much less the right one. A common one is the desire for a major that the college doesn't offer, since students often change their interests. Often it's the desire to be in or near a city, or to be in a larger place. There is so much movement among institutions that one reason has to be that freshmen and sophomores often think the grass is greener on the other side of the fence. Freshmen may also say something akin to, "Half the freshman class is transferring out." Go to the registrar and ask how many requests he's had for transcripts to be sent to other institutions; maybe it'll be three or four. If dissatisfaction with the quality of the school comes to be the major reason, more specific inquiries will give you an indication whether you'd be unhappy too.

■ What is the attrition rate? Some state institutions have lost as many as 80 percent of their freshmen in four years; in others 30 percent or more of the students don't return for the sophomore year. The popular University of Colorado graduates only 40 percent in four years. At the other end of the scale, some colleges graduate 80 or 90 percent of an entering class, and in between, a lot of good colleges lose 40 percent or more over four years. It is worthwhile finding out why students leave; it may be because they don't have the commitment to learning expected in that community; it may be because they want more bodies around; or it may not be a very good place. You will have to decide whether the reasons are relevant to you.

■ What kind of rapport is there between students and faculty? This is a key question. The ideal learning situation is one in which the student is heavily involved, not just a receptive ear. If there is the kind of close collaboration—and stimulus—that makes this possible, that fact will come out loud and clear. The students will refer to faculty members as valued mentors, bull-session participants, or advisers. If you see faculty members having coffee with students or meandering across campus with them, these are good signs.

■ Does the school have good faculty people across the board, not just in the major you think you want?

■ Are there special opportunities, like off-campus programs, especially foreign study, doing research with a faculty member, or independent study, readily available, or are they just on paper?

■ Does every senior have to write a thesis or do some major project as a capstone of his college experience? This is very important. It is a major clue both to the quality of the learning experience and to the depth of student-faculty relations.

■ Ask a dozen or more students: If you came back here after graduation, would you have good enough faculty friends that you might have dinner or spend a night at one of their homes? In a good undergraduate college most of the answers will be yes, or there's something wrong. In a large school that question is more likely to provide laughter, although at Washington University in St. Louis I asked twenty-two students that question and got twenty affirmative answers.

■ Who does the teaching? If graduate assistants teach the required general education courses, freshmen and sophomores are being cheated. If they're taught by senior faculty but in auditorium-size classes, that's still shortchanging the students because it's only a lecture. Graduate students are, with mighty few exceptions, untrained, unsupervised mercenaries working on their own advanced degrees. Their primary interest is in their own degree, not yours, and they constitute a way of saving money at the expense of the undergraduate.

■ How many part-time teachers are there?

■ Are there any foreign teachers whose English is so poor they are hard to understand? A federal survey found that over 43 percent of all university faculty members are part-time, many of them aliens, unfamiliar with our culture or language. If there are a lot of part-time faculty, that is a black mark, for the temporary teacher has little or no loyalty or commitment to the school. He may be hard to find after class, and as an academic adviser worse than useless; as one student told a member of a survey team visiting colleges, "They don't know how the college works."

■ Is there any TV or programmed instruction where no instructor meets the class?

■ What are class sizes, really? The institution may advertise a low student-faculty ratio, but don't buy that. Ask particularly about the courses that all or most freshmen or sophomores have to take.

■ Are there any classes of one hundred? And if so, how many? The answers will reveal pretty starkly an important difference between the college and the large university.

■ Do faculty make themselves available after class and keep regular office hours, or do they vanish? At Cornell

University, for example, faculty members commonly take refuge in the graduate library, where undergraduates are not permitted. At many urban institutions they hurry home to the suburbs. In a small college town or on the campus of a small college, there is no place for either student or teacher to hide.

■ Does the faculty advising system really work? This is where practically every college fails at least some of the time. Do the advisers really advise, with a knowledge of the student's background and interests, or do they just initial class schedules? The answers will tell something about student-faculty relationships, which are crucial. Advising doesn't necessarily mean job counseling; that is the placement office's function. Undergraduates need help in understanding that their education is preparing them for a lifetime of work—and fulfillment—not just for a first job. A rapidly changing world has made mature advice on why they're there, what they are getting for princely tuitions, and how those courses will fit them for the world of work matters of far greater moment than they were forty or fifty years ago. And if students don't get some such advice, they'll rightly think they've been gypped.

Two of the requisites of a good college experience are two continuing conversations. One is with your teachers, who ought to be mature individuals, competent in their fields, with a broad view of the world and an interest in the student. The second conversation, with your peers, is a part of the process of internal exploration that college should be. The two together help in shaping values, attitudes, and aspirations, and are as crucial as the standards and the expectations of the classroom. The course content is something that evaporates over time.

■ What is the learning atmosphere? Is learning the concern, or grades? Is there intense competition for grades?

■ Is cheating common, or is there an ethos or an honor code that condemns it?

■ Is this a demanding or an easy place? A college may be easy or difficult to get into, but the central consideration is rigor. One may be a lot tougher to get into than to stay in, while another that's easy to get into may be more demanding. If it's easy, it's a sham. And it's a simple matter to find out by asking a few students how many hours a week they study, how many pages they read a night, and what the level of expectation is.

■ Is it possible to study in your dorm rooms? Noisy dorms are not just an inconvenience; they are cause to shun the place. If there are no quiet hours, it means learning is not very important here. Fun and games come first.

■ What percentage of students leave campus on weekends? If it's a suitcase college, the parking lots become deserted Thursday afternoon or Friday, and the sense of community is diluted or nonexistent. If most everybody clears out every weekend, that also says something about the amount of work expected.

■ What is the social life like? Are there dominant social groups, such as fraternities, and if so, is it easy to move among them, or are they tightly cloistered? Is it possible to be editor of the paper or class president and not be a member?

■ Are athletics only for the hired jocks, or do a substantial number of the paying students have the fun of playing on varsity and intramural teams? In other words, is the big football weekend the only athletic event the student body takes an interest in?

■ Is there a variety of campus activities and imported speakers, music, and other cultural events? In most good colleges, the answers to that question are affirmative; in fact, many campuses offer more such variety than the nearby town or city.

■ Do the students take advantage of these activities? This often destroys the frequent complaint that "there's nothing to do here." And of course it says something about the students.

■ What is the drinking, drug, and sex scene? Would a person of your beliefs be comfortable here?

■ Does the place favor anonymity and conformity, or does it encourage identity and individualism? Does it coddle or challenge? Colleges will differ startlingly.

Teenagers often say they don't want to be a number in a big school, or just as often say they don't want a college smaller than their suburban high school. The fear of being a number may mask apprehensions about competing with a dauntingly large number of very able peers, while wanting a college larger than your high school may reveal fear of the close scrutiny you might get as a person in a college with high expectations where everyone is clearly visible and weighed. But just about every grade-A undergraduate college is smaller than the suburban high school.

As a visitor, you should come to terms with yourself on this score, because a principal benefit of a good college is finding out who you are and what you want to become, and maybe taking a step or two on the road toward becoming that kind of person. As the catalog of the exciting but late lamented Kirkland College—now absorbed by Hamilton—once said, "College is a time of internal exploration and the small, familial community is more conducive to that."

Wanting a major the college doesn't offer is frequently a cause of transferring, and often as not it is not a good reason. For one thing, most students change majors at least once. For another, only about one person in ten is doing anything at age fifty that she was interested in as a freshman. And again, she should be getting a good broad education now; specialization should come later.

■ How easy is it to get the classes you want at registration? Or is it even possible?

Questions to Ask Faculty and Administrators

■ What happens to graduates? What percentage goes on to graduate and professional schools? What percentage goes into business or teaching?

■ Does the college have a good career counseling office and placement director that works closely with students *throughout* their college days, not just at the end? The career counseling office should complement and supplement the faculty adviser. Does his office have a good pipeline to the job market?

■ What has been the graduates' record in getting jobs, what kinds, where, and at what salary levels?

■ What is the record in graduate and professional school acceptance?

■ Does the college take a healthy pride in itself, or is it so smugly sure of itself as to be chauvinistic?

■ Does it have a "reject morale" because it was a fallback or a safety school for a number of the students?

■ Ask the librarian about the extent of library usage. It may be nearly empty during the middle of the day and crowded early in the morning or at night. Are more students playing the pinball or video game machines in the student center than are using the library?

■ Ask faculty members what they think of the students, how they compare them with students at other places they've taught. And ask them what percentages of the ones they teach are interested in learning.

College should be a place of diverse people and views and beliefs. It should be a place where faculty takes an interest in campus programs outside of the classroom. It should be a place of debate, questioning, and discussion. It should have a feeling of family or community.

When you visit, you are the customer. Any question that is important to you deserves a full and candid answer. If, with a reasonable effort, you don't get it, that's a black mark against the school, but the chances are you'll get more than you expected.

CHAPTER 12

Judging Yourself as an Applicant

UNLESS YOU'RE DETERMINED TO TWIST your nervous system out of shape by getting into the elite school rat race (to no good end), you shouldn't have much trouble, regardless of what you read in the newspapers and magazines. And that applies whether you're an A or a B student, in some cases even lower.

There are a lot of transforming but unselective small colleges among the more than two thousand in the country, and they will do more to make you a more effective and better person than any of the Ivies or their clones. Guaranteed.

A good place to start looking is by reading *Colleges That Change Lives: Forty Schools That Will Change the Way You Think about Colleges*. The colleges featured here all have track records of producing effective, moral adults, which is the college's

job. There are colleges for all kinds, from the naïf to the intellectual (most of the few truly intellectual schools are not selective). And they want you! That's why they're in the book.

Why is all this true? Because selectivity is the creature of
the GI Bill and the explosion of college-going that over-
whelmed the higher education establishment after World
War II. Before that, every college—even Harvard—had a mix
of abilities; the middle students asked the questions that the
top students were afraid or ashamed to ask, and that the
Gentlemen's Cs didn't think of. When everyone is a top student, as a transfer from Wesleyan told me, "it's stifling, but at
Beloit everyone is so open. Beloit may not have the prestige,
but the learning is better." Even at intellectual St. John's,
Dean Eva Brann told me, "Some of the most useful questions are asked by the weaker students."

You should keep in mind three things: colleges exagger-
ate their GPAs and SATs; academic aptitude is only a tiny
sliver of intelligence, much smaller than emotional intelligence; and third, most famous people have not been top
students.

A famous scientist, Rita Levi-Montalcini, founder of
Rome's Laboratory of Cell Biology, looking back on her long
life and those of her peers and colleagues, says that the keys
to personal success and fulfillment are neither "the degree of
intelligence nor the ability to carry out one's tasks with thor-
oughness and precision." More important, she says, are total
dedication and a tendency to underestimate difficulties,
"which cause one to tackle problems that other, more critical
and acute persons instead opt to avoid."

There's nothing new about all this; Moses complained to
the Lord that he not only was a slow learner but had a speech

impediment—learning-disabled, we'd call it today. George Washington wasn't famed as an intellectual, nor was Harry Truman. But all three of them did pretty well. It's just as I've been saying everywhere I could: motivation and desire fuel the bold, successful life. Or, as Ecclesiastes puts it, "Again I saw that under the sun the race is not to the swift . . . nor riches to the intelligent . . . but time and chance happen to them all." And both time and chance tilt toward those with dedication and desire.

Such dramatic stuff is folk knowledge to admissions people. As the late Bill Wilson of Amherst responded to a successful young man he had rejected ten years earlier, "I wish I had a nickel for every Pulitzer Prize winner I've turned down." And one of his famous colleagues, Alden Thresher of MIT, advocated choosing freshman classes by random selection, since all the applicants were qualified. (The wise Mr. Thresher, however, didn't propose making admissions officers technologically obsolete until he'd retired.) In the college-going rush of the 1950s, the president of Michigan State reportedly told his admissions office at one point to accept the next hundred applicants that came in, no exceptions. The story is that this group did just as well as those selected by the wisdom of the admissions staff.

Random selection is still proposed every once in a while as the only fair way for the highly selective colleges to choose their freshman classes, and for very good reasons. While it is central to admissions mythology that the keepers of the gates are judging and rewarding individual merit, the track records of their picks show them to be poor handicappers. As evidence elsewhere in this book shows, there is a startling lack of correlation between selectivity and alumni achievement.

There are two solid reasons why the elite schools' gate-keepers don't and can't judge merit. One is that their real purpose is to admit the applicants they think can help the school achieve its own political, social, athletic, and status goals. And status is the most precious goal of all. Under truth serum almost any highly selective college director would admit he's afraid to have a high school counselor see him take anyone with a verbal score under 600. He'd be branded as willing to take the lesser students. Anyone who scores in the middle 400s on the verbal part of the SATs can do the work at any college, and study after study has underscored the common knowledge that there's no connection between college grades and later achievement—except for mathematicians, who are born, not made.

One of those studies, by psychologists at Harvard, Boston, and Wesleyan, found that the most outstanding students in college are the ones most likely to be unhappy ten years after graduation. And there was absolutely no correlation between scholastic achievement and later getting top jobs, high income, or similar accomplishments.

Another, by Dr. Douglas Heath of Haverford, went further. He found that those with the best college records were less mature and less competent ten to fifteen years later than those of modest academic success. They tended to be more self-centered and had "tense and distant" relationships at work, and "less intimate relationships with their wives" at home. In short, the academic world is putting its highest valuations on the wrong people for the wrong reasons. They are ignoring character, the development of which should be central to the mission of liberal education. It follows then that by using academic statistics as the principal measures of worth, the admissions people are not serving the public good if they lack the moral compasses.

The other reason is that no one has yet found an acceptable way to describe merit; much less, how to decide whether one ability or talent is better than another.

It is not unusual to hear admissions officers say that most of the personal statements they read are boring, dull, or wimpishly playing it safe. A former Yale admissions director told me they're all bland. So why was Yale admitting them? What good for the individual or for the virility of a nation was its selection process accomplishing? Are the admissions staffs serving a democratic society well? They're playing it safe, protecting themselves. The whole situation calls to mind a successful author's efforts to warn a would-be freelance writer about another group that plays it safe: "Every editor ought to be horsewhipped every day in the public square."

So, the message is that if you're turned down by one school, consider the source; it's not a verdict on your quality, your ability, or your prospects in life, no matter how much it hurts your ego. It means only that you're not getting into that academic club. Take heart: equally good schools are looking for you, schools you someday may be urging your own kids to consider.

If You're Learning-Disabled

A learning disability does not bar success in college. On the contrary, it may contribute to success in college and after. The dyslexics and the problem learners of other kinds, having had to work to conquer or compensate for some handicap or disability, usually have more motivation to succeed, and that's 95 percent of the battle almost anywhere.

Several years ago I had a client who'd graduated from a New England prep school in spite of a bad case of dyslexia that had not been discovered—unbelievable as that seems—until he was in the eleventh grade. He worked hard at a compensatory program and graduated from a very good college. Another boy whose disability was such that, from the age of twelve to fifteen, he'd been in an exceedingly costly private school for dyslexics insisted on getting into the public school mainstream as a junior because "in the special school people weren't working." By his senior year he was getting As and Bs in a fairly competitive suburban high school. His highest SAT verbal score was 370, but his math was an unusual 700. After completing three years at St. Andrews Presbyterian with a 3.7 average, he went to Georgia Tech for the engineering part of a 3–2 program and graduated summa cum laude with a 3.6 average. That is half of the story. As a senior, he passed the PhD entrance exam, something half of the master's degree candidates fail. He won a teaching fellowship and his master's degree. In June 1994, Rockwell International, which had laid off 40,000 people, and was being five times as picky as the year before, hiring 1,000 engineers in 1993 but only 200 in 1994, hired him as an electrical engineer at $42,000.

In a quarter century I have seen kids with every kind of disability you can think of—brain damage from leukemia therapy, blindness, and the many manifestations of dyslexia—go to college and prosper. But whatever the problem, they had one thing in common: they worked at it, and thereby overcame or compensated for it.

My most dramatic case was one that sparkles with the extra-thyroid energy and determination that Emerson had in mind when he wrote, "What will you have, quoth God. Pay for it and take it." In the winter of 1988 this student graduated from American University with a 2.5 average, all the while running a very successful home construction business. But four years earlier, he started his college application essay with these exact words: "Dyslexia is a problem which has hovered over me for the entirety of my life."

When he started working with a tutor in the eleventh grade, he said,

> I would read something and not understand a word of it. . . . I would have to read every word with a teacher. Even then I might not understand a word of it. . . . I would review the material until I reached a point of exhaustion. . . . By my sophomore year, however, I was doing the initial work myself with only guidance and correction from others. At present I am able to independently read a work such as *Hamlet*, comprehend the plot, and respond to questions. Skills at this level have made it possible for me to maintain a C+ average in a college prep school despite my learning disability.

Those skills were the fruit of dogged effort. He spent ten hours on his *Hamlet* report, but he wrote it without any help. His SAT verbal went from 370 in 1983 to 470 in 1984.

If you think he harbored any self-doubts, consider this: he applied to eighteen colleges, six of which were grade-A schools I had talked to about him. He got acceptances from sixteen, was wait-listed at one, and was rejected by only one!

Of course, admissions officers were sure he would pay the price.

Another fellow whose eyesight was so poor that he had been judged legally blind made much use of tapes and talking books. In the tenth grade he decided he wanted to go to college, worked harder, raised his grades from Cs and Ds to Bs and Cs, and his verbal score rose 100 points. He did well enough at Hiram College that he won a graduate fellowship to Carnegie-Mellon. Another example is that of a girl, blind from birth, who won honors in French at the University of Rochester.

Whoever You Are

Lay all the cards on the table. Don't try to hide anything, whatever the problem—learning, financial, family crisis, your sins, or anything else. Admissions people have common sense and want to help.

Don't underestimate yourself if you're a B student; most of the world's good work is done by B (and C) students. A lot of very good colleges want you.

If you're a hotshot student, don't overestimate yourself; straight-A and 1500 SAT (old scale) applicants are a dime a dozen, and they're all applying to the same schools.

You're approaching one of the most crucial decisions of your life, and it deserves a good deal of effort from you. Look up colleges on the Internet. By all means visit them and ask the questions important to you. Whatever your GPA, there are more colleges interested in you than you think, but they do not buy a pig in a poke. You're preparing for the rest of your life, maybe half a century or a couple of decades longer!

Don't think the name of your high school carries any special leverage (unless it's one of the many clones of the Bronx High School of Science). Your competition comes from very smart kids in the good suburban high schools across the country.

Whoever you are, remember that it's not an admissions committee that makes the real judgment on you; it will always be you.

CHAPTER 13

Should Parents Let Their Child Take a Year Off?

PARENTS DON'T EVEN LIKE TO think about such a prospect; it gives them the willies. If a student is already doing less than he should, or than they think he should, they fear a year away from school will surely nudge him over the brink and down the slippery slope. And if he is going along all right, they're afraid the interruption will break the spell. The pronoun is masculine because the male of the species is the one most likely to be getting terrible grades or wanting to get off the conveyor belt for a while to look around.

The good news is that a year off will be the salvation of the underachiever and the focusing and firming of the one who wants off for a while—*if* there is a plan, and *if* it is followed. This salvation is not, like the hereafter, a matter of faith. The efficacy of taking a year off is a demonstrated fact of adolescent metamorphosis. As you'll see later, it's been working like magic, so far as college performance is concerned, for forty years. When I was a college administrator I wanted to impose a year off, working, on every class of high school seniors before they came to college. The idea was a pipe dream, of course, but after a year out working they would be a different group, more mature, and chomping at the bit. Consequently, they would tend to get a lot more out of college.

The bad news is that if parents chicken out and don't insist that their son follow his plan, if they let him lounge around the house and sponge off them, they not only will make things worse, they'll interfere with his growing up by providing a crutch instead of a push. More bad news is that parents too often are bleeding hearts, unable to stick with the plan.

There is only one caveat: a few people never do grow up. However, making them accept some responsibility will help; otherwise their tendency to lean will be encouraged.

Having a plan is absolutely essential. The youth's days should be occupied with a full-time job or a serious project; no hanging around the house watching television, driving the car, and living off the parents. The time will have to be accounted for when he does apply to college. Every admissions director will demand it; there's no skipping or forgetting the year, although many think or hope this will be the case.

If the year has been idled away doing nothing, the admissions director will be inclined to say, "Go take some courses; prove that you're ready to work." His rationale will rightly be that the person who spends a term or a year doing nothing is not likely to be motivated to do much in college either.

Who Should Take a Year Off?

The too-simple answer is a person in one of two categories. In one is the person who feels very strongly he wants to do so and persists in it over a period of many months, and who has a definite plan or a sensible reason he can explain. In the other category is someone whose attitude and performance should make it clear that he has no desire to do, and will not do, the work.

In the first case, if a high school senior very much wants to take a year off, it is counterproductive for parents to push for college. Forcing him to go anyway breeds apathy or unhappiness, and the usual consequences are poor performance and failure. I have seen it happen time after time; indeed, it seems to me that the unhappy students I've encountered are the results of either uninformed choice or parental interference, where parents either refuse to let them take a year off or insist on an unwanted college choice, or sometimes both. When someone really has his heart and soul set on taking a year off, that will be pretty clear.

But remember that adolescents' attitudes are as changeable as the wind; I've know many youngsters to say in the winter—especially if their grades are bad—that they don't want to go to college the following year. But by spring or summer, when friends are all making their college plans, they suddenly have the urge. And they go.

This changeability makes it important to keep the options open until late summer by going through the selection and application process anyway.

In the other category, when high school grades have been dropping from alarming to catastrophic, and the senior grades are all Fs and Ds, a year off working and supporting himself may make college an investment rather than a bad-odds gamble. But here we leave solid ground, because the youth may have more than the usual problems of this most tortured period of life. It could be a divorce, an alcoholic parent, refusal to compete with a sibling or parent, or an alien social world. He may need sympathetic and perceptive counseling, or a change of venue—getting into a supportive college setting where he can have a successful experience. And the word *successful* is crucial.

However, just because a teenager doesn't seem to do a darn thing about selecting colleges or filling out applications doesn't necessarily mean that he's in the not-ready category. Every late winter and spring, parents echo one doctor's angry threat of a few years ago: "This boy isn't going to college next fall, he's just not ready. He hasn't done a darn thing about filling out a single application!" But his son went that fall and did beautifully. Parents forget that the male adolescent's planning span is only about twelve hours.

A fifth year of high school isn't likely to do the nonperformer—or the parents' peace of mind—a bit of good; he'll be bored and just as unproductive. Nor is sending him to the local community college the answer. There he'd be exposed to the same distractions and temptations as high school; in addition, since it's a commuter school and the end of the educational line for most of its students, the atmosphere is anything but inspiring or conducive to work. Let him get a job and see how the other half lives and how limited his prospects are!

The following story of a college flunkout, his conversion and salvation, should be an object lesson to parents. This intelligent, likable young man had been a sinner longer than most and expressed himself more eloquently, but his story has universality.

In high school he had a 2.7 average but was capable of a 3.5 or better. After four semesters in an ill-chosen college he was on academic warning; the next semester he was suspended for a term. Later in his junior year he was dismissed for a full year. He went home, got a job as a cook, and had no intention of going back to college, for he soon got a raise, and within six months had been made supervisor of the restaurant. In less than eight months he was in my office with his parents, wanting to get back into college.

As he said, "There is no challenge; I'm not fulfilled; my life is empty. My friends are intelligent, open-minded, curious, with a sense of adventure; but these people I can't even talk to. All they can see in life is getting a BMW or a Jaguar. I wish now I'd gotten out [of college] earlier. But it was a free ride; I had money, a place to live and have fun and go to class occasionally. I was the life of the party. Now I want to do these essential things: go to class, read, read over my notes, learn."

His parents, one a graduate of Duke, the other of Yale with a doctorate in physics from Chicago, both held executive positions, but neither shook a finger at him. As long as they were willing to keep on giving, he was happy to keep on taking. It took the mental shock of exposure to the world to wake him up.

He was able to get a glowing recommendation from his boss. He convinced me that he had been affected by maturity's magic, if long overdue, spell, and I was thereby able to convince an admissions director or two, with the result that he got into a first-rate college, where he gave a good account of himself. He will in life, too, as do the others who are thus born again, for they have learned a lesson the hard way.

Here the admissions directors should get a bow for taking a chance, as several of them over the years have, on a risk venture who with his less-than-C average was not legal tender in the academic world. I've never had a repentant flunkout who didn't get another chance from at least one good school.

What Kind of a Job Is Good?

The quality of the job is not important except in a negative sense, as the foregoing story exemplifies: the more menial the job, the better the therapy. A dull, tedious, or difficult job that is mentally numbing drives home the lesson that if you don't want to continue to live like the other half does, you'd better do something about exploiting your abilities. That's not to say that if you accomplish something noteworthy, like being promoted to reporter from copy boy, as one young friend did, it won't help get you into Amherst in spite of an indifferent high school record.

If Not a Job, What Kind of Project Is Acceptable?

One can pursue a hobby or a business of one's own, travel, take a study abroad program, take courses—in fact do almost anything, but the operative word is *do*.

What Does the College Want to Know about the Year Off?

If it's been a job, the kind of work record is very important because the boss can testify to your attitude and performance, which will be as good as a teacher's recommendation, as the college flunkout's story shows.

If it's been some other plan, the admissions people will want to know exactly what you did and why and what you accomplished, if anything.

What you can say you learned from your year off is equally important. If a student has looked at himself, it will reveal to what extent that secret ingredient, the process called maturing, has affected him. It produces changes for the good, partly because it not only gives a young person time to take stock of his situation but also, since he can't go to school for a term or a year, enforces a waiting period for resolutions on the new life to firm and set. When I see a client after a year off working or doing something with a purpose, he's a different person; his eye seems clearer and more direct, his handshake is firmer, his voice is more positive, he has a goal, and most important of all, he has motivation, which is 95 percent of the battle.

In short, a year out in the world teaches a hard lesson and teaches it well and for good; namely, that the unprepared brain is sentenced to the have-not jobs. The frustrations and the ego bruises help the maturing process, unfailingly making converts of the doubters and unbelievers.

How Can Parents Be Sure of All This?

There is plenty of evidence that the young subject wises up. The first great revelation came after World War II, when returning GIs by the thousands made uniformly good records in college, irrespective of how bad their high school grades had been. Almost no one flunked out. It was so dramatic a showing that the vice president of Pennsylvania State University campaigned to have Congress require military service right after high school so as to let youths mature before going to college. He argued that the more mature, motivated students would get more out of college, and the school and the taxpayer would benefit as well from the improved efficiency.

As a result of this dramatic experience with returning veterans, several of the most prestigious colleges made it a practice in the late 1950s and early 1960s (when there was a plethora of college applicants) to compel students who weren't doing as well as they should to take a year off, without prejudice, to mature. They always came back.

Several studies have been done more recently on those who drop out once they're in college. At Harvard it was found that most of them returned and earned their degrees. This is what happens with most middle- and upper-middle-class students. It is the students from lower-income families who tend to stay out because the problem is money.

What If a Student Doesn't Want to Go to College After a Year Off?

In the rare case of a youth who simply does not want to go to college, the parent might just as well take a deep breath, relax, acquiesce, and wait for time to do its work, which may take another year or more. But the parents must insist that he get a job and support himself, or else the battle will be prolonged or lost. If he goes to college against his will, the odds are that he will do poorly or flunk out; and with a poor record, he will have trouble later on getting into a place he might like. If he stays out and works, he will find, sooner or later, that he'd better get the credentials or be doomed to second-class citizenship in the job world.

Does This Happen Often?

Parents who confront the problem of a child who drops out or who refuses to go think it is a shame that only they bear, a dread social disease. It might comfort them to know that it's the biggest club in the country. Sometimes it seems half the families in the country must have one child who has seceded from the Establishment. At dinner one night with former clients whose oldest son had covered himself with academic honors from Princeton on to a doctorate, and whose youngest son had graduated from a prestige college, the conversation was largely about the family trauma over the middle child, a girl who had been a hard-core dropout and a runaway. But she had finally graduated from college. The father said, "I learned three things from that experience: There's nothing you can do about it. It's not your fault. And they do come back." A soft sculpture with that message, done by the artist mother, hung on a wall in my office. As I exclaimed at the time, "I've been trying to tell parents that for fifteen years!"

What If Someone Never Goes to College?

Of course, many people make notable contributions or achieve great success in many different fields without ever setting foot on a college campus, or getting a degree. The late great Bill Wilson, longtime Amherst admissions dean, was fond of saying that probably 20 percent of the real achievers in this country never set foot on a college campus. But they are usually the people with an idea or a cause that drives them, and perhaps an extra thyroid gland. They fashion their own educations in their own ways or as adult students.

One of the more dramatic examples was Nicholas Christofilos, the Greek creator of America's atom smasher and discoverer of the natural radiation belts encircling the earth—now known as the Van Allen radiation belts—among other spectacular feats. He won the Franklin Institute's Elliot Cresson Medal for his contributions to nuclear physics. He was not only largely self-taught in physics, but also had to invent his own mathematics to present his atom smasher principle. Three years after American scientists at the Brookhaven National Laboratory had pooh-poohed his ideas as unworkable—they couldn't understand his math— they finally came up with the same idea. Christofilos was the star of the American nuclear physics team until his death in 1972.

So parents shouldn't be too worried; if their child doesn't have the drive of an extra thyroid gland, he'll soon see that getting the credentials is really the primrose path. If he does have the drive, he either won't need the credentials, or he'll get 'em in his own way.

CHAPTER 14

A Good Application = Open Sesame

A STATEMENT THAT REVEALS who you are can often work wonders.

Believe it or not, a C student, and sometimes a D student, can write as effective an application as a valedictorian, often a better one. How so? Because the honest, self-revealing one is persuasive; sometimes it can even win an acceptance over better SAT scores and grades. But the cute, smart, affected, or phony one gags the bored reader and tilts that folder toward the reject pile.

You don't have to be a talented writer, but you have to know your subject: yourself. You should feel strongly about what you're saying, whether the topic is frivolous or serious, and you must say it sensibly and grammatically. Also, it is absolutely crucial to write for an audience of one: yourself. Then it will have the eloquence of honesty. If it's written with an eye to "What do they want?" you're dead. "They" want to know who you are, and you'll never be able to tell them if you're looking at them instead of yourself. All you'll do is defeat your purpose and turn off the reader.

Unless it's something that's been simmering on the back burner of your mind for some time and just comes to a boil, you're probably going to have to redo your application a couple of times at least to make it say what you want it to say. Every professional writer has to rewrite and rewrite: why should you expect to get it right the first time? The human brain works slowly; as the *New Yorker*'s famed James Thurber explained, "I'm not a writer; I'm a rewriter." A very good high school debater, now a Harvard alumnus, rewrote his statement three times before he was telling why he debated, rather than what he had achieved, which was already in the data part of his application.

The whole purpose of the essays is to provide a glimpse of you as a person, to give insight that the objective data do not. That glimpse gets points for being well thought out and well written, and gets marked down for being sloppily handled. The assigned topics test your imagination, thinking, and writing ability. These two personal parts give you the chance to set yourself apart from the rest of that great pile of folders, to make your application come alive. When you're in a competitive situation, at least half of those thousands of folders will have as good or better statistics and credentials, whether you want to think so or not. That means that what you say about yourself is crucial. The interview is nothing by comparison—in fact, many of the most competitive places would like to eliminate them, or pay them little mind. When you've performed below your ability, or for some other reason consider yourself a late bloomer, what you say about yourself can save you or hang you.

On the personal statement essay (the question that asks you to tell something about yourself that you want the college to know), imagine you're responding to a pen pal from another land or civilization wanting to know what makes you tick, what's important to you, how you live. There are no holds barred; as Horton the elephant said in Dr. Seuss's book *Horton Hatches an Egg*, "I say what I mean and I mean what I say." No matter how far out the topic or viewpoint, if it's genuine and supported it will be effective, even when it flaunts the arrogance of youth. When Bennington College was at its peak of selectivity a good many years back, a client was asking me what she should say in her application, because, she explained, "I really don't know what college can teach me." The next time I had occasion to call Bennington, an incredulous admissions director asked me, "Do you know what [that girl] said in her application?" Bennington accepted her.

Another client whose only activity was crew coxswain is proof positive that the essay is often the deciding factor. She and a classmate who had better grades and more impressive activities both applied to Harvard and Swarthmore. And this was the year Swarthmore was called the best college in the country by the *US News and World Report* rating. Her classmate was accepted at Harvard but rejected by Swarthmore. My client was accepted at both. The difference had to be the essay. It was about a personal tragedy, alopecia, and how she handled it. We had several conferences and she revised it several times, always to delete words, not add them. She went to Swarthmore.

Here is her essay:

THE BALD AND THE BEAUTIFUL

"I'm shedding," I said casually one day, as I ran my fingers through my hair and several strands came out painlessly. As a naïve third-grader, I was quite proud of the fact that it didn't hurt when I pulled my own hair out. For a few days it was a joke; I would let classmates take turns grabbing at my hair, and I'd smile when they'd marvel at how easily it left my scalp. The joke lost a fraction of its humor each day, though, as my hairline quickly receded. I attempted to hide my hair loss by sporting thick headbands when my bangs fell out, and baseball caps when the bare spots were evident. I cried myself to sleep on countless nights. After a peaceful slumber, I would wake to the same harsh situation—hundreds of hairs on my pillow where my head had rested, and tears from the night before caked on my cheeks. Only one month later, the head under my curly brunette wig was completely bald.

I was diagnosed with alopecia—entire hair loss—and reality was suddenly thrust upon me: I had no hair and there was nothing I could do about it. Why couldn't I be normal like my friends? Why did I have to be bald? What would people say about me? I informed only my closest friends of the situation, and begged them not to tell anyone; if the word got out, I wouldn't be able to show my face in school again. I tried to assure myself that the secret was safe with my friends, but in the back of my mind I knew it wasn't. Whenever I observed a quiet conversation between classmates, I sensed that they were talking about me. If someone happened to look at me as I walked to class, my heart would race; I would worry for the rest of the day whether or not that person realized I wore a wig. Watching my friends grow up—seemingly without major problems—was unnerving to me. Everyone was perfect and I was bald.

I would have no hair for the next five years. Although this long period began dismally, I matured and found that my imperfection was definitely not fit to mourn over. I firmly decided to live my life to the fullest and come out of my ashamed seclusion. My self-consciousness gave way to strong self-confidence and I grew happier and emotionally stronger. If I could overcome my baldness, nothing could stand in my way. On the first day of eighth grade I attended school without the comfort of a wig—for the first time in five years. I finally conquered the insecure mentality that had so injured my self-esteem. Every day with hair would be a wonderful day.

My struggle with alopecia transformed me from a shy and self-conscious little girl into an open and self-assured young woman. I was once so reserved that I detached myself from my surroundings; now I am much happier being involved in many activities. I've been an officer of a school community service club, a coxswain of the crew team, and a co-captain of the tennis team—feats I couldn't have dreamed of at the onset of my alopecia. While I had a difficult time coping with my condition, conquering it was the boost I needed to propel me to face new challenges. Although alopecia can be recurring, I do not fear going bald a second time. If I lose my hair again, I'll be ready to face my condition head-on, armed with an unconquerable confidence.

Two Important Things to Do Before Starting an Essay

1. Do the self-examination suggested in chapter 10, "What Are You Going For, Really?" That will get your thinking on track and very likely suggest a topic.

2. Read the second and the last chapters of *The Elements of Style* by Strunk and White. This magic little book is the best thing ever written on how to use your mother tongue effectively. The principles in those thirty-seven small pages are worth more than everything else that's ever been or is now being written on the subject of college application essays. They will put up road signs for you; they will keep you out of the ditch, and prevent you from crossing the double yellow lines.

How Long Does It Have to Be?

Just long enough to make your point, and no longer. If the instructions say to keep it within a certain space, do so. Otherwise, try to do it in two hundred words; it will be more effective than if you take four hundred. There's a hoary newspaperman's saying that goes: "I didn't have time to write a short story." The long one is the verbose, easily written one. See the two gems under "Assigned Topic."

One Central Thing to Keep in Mind While Writing

Use the whats to hang the whys onto. And be specific about them; give the details. A general statement not supported is bad writing. Only damage is done by writing such things as, "My trip exposed me to other cultures," or "I learned the value of hard work from my victory." You may think these are true and profound, but your reader will only gag. You don't have to beat your breast; the data have already recorded your feats or failures. This is where you explain why you did it, or why it meant something to you, or what it did for you, or why you sinned, and whether and why you've changed. When you do this, you're giving the reader a feeling for you as a human being, which is what he wants.

After You've Written a Draft

Read it aloud to see how it sounds; if it sounds queer or stiff, it is.

Rework it and ask a friend to read it. An unbiased opinion is valuable, and a friend is usually better for this than a parent, who tends to be too emotionally involved in the project, and often much too cautious, as we will see further on.

There Are No Bad Topics, But—

There are only bad ways of handling topics. You can avoid emptiness, pretension, cuteness (clever is fine *if* it's the real thing), and other sins by writing honestly and imaginatively about something important to you, no matter how trivial. But it has to be something that only you could write, because you're telling, in specific detail, what it did to you. Generalizations that anyone could write are not just useless, they're boring.

Don't write about your trip unless you have something more specific and less pretentious to say than "I have had the thrilling adventure of exploring a variety of landscapes from the tumultuous terrain of Alaska to the mystic fjords of Norway. . . . Travel . . . has deepened perception, broadened imagination, sharpened sensitivity, and refined the intellect." As Jeannette Hersey, former Connecticut College admissions director, said of personal essays, "Ninety-five percent of them are travelogues." They tell where the applicant has been or what she has done, but not why she did it or precisely what she got from it.

Here are excerpts from one that Jeannette Hersey or anyone else would rank high in the good 5 percent, because this travel obviously did do something to the intellect:

The first few years of my life were spent in the suburbs of Washington, D.C., where I attended a small private boys' school. I was no more concerned with my future then than any young American kid whose main interests were in collecting baseball cards and chasing the Good Humor man. . . . My life dramatically changed, however, when my family moved to Yarmouth, Nova Scotia. . . . Suddenly, I was thrust from a suburban American lifestyle to that of a rural Canadian town of 8,000. At the outset I was shocked, but gradually began to understand and appreciate the differences between Yarmouth and Washington. . . . I have never met as many generous, caring, and trusting people. . . . Even something as simple as yielding right-of-way to pedestrians at an intersection is a reflection of the unhurried lifestyle that allows time for the consideration of others. The smallness of the town causes everyone to know everyone, and thus engenders a trust for others. It is, therefore, not unusual to find a clothing store manager who would sell you a pair of pants even if you were a few dollars short, knowing you would pay him later. . . . This . . . lifestyle was very secure . . . and even for those who left it, the town became a retreat from the outside world they often found difficult to adjust to. . . . Most were never motivated to achieve a higher socio-economic status than the previous generation because it often required leaving the "nest." The end result for some were lives that revolved around a six-foot slab of sidewalk in front of the Main Street pharmacy. . . . "Why should I work hard in school? My dad and brothers have never gone anywhere in life," asked one of my closest friends whose father was an alcoholic fisherman. I could sympathize with his lack of motivation and differing goals, but it was hard for me to accept his failing in school and thus I spent many tutorial hours helping him make the grade. . . . However, it would be a mistake to criticize the whole town as being without motivation. Their priorities were merely different, and success in many cases was not measured on an individual basis. . . . There was no greater disappointment than having rain on the day of a community picnic that had been planned for over a month. Nor for me was there any greater pleasure than witnessing the smile on an old canoe craftsman's face after his donated canoe was raffled off in support of the local fire department. In reflecting on my experience, I was often forced to ask the perplexing question, "What is success?" It had always seemed reasonable to equate success with happiness or peace of mind. . . . This revelation forced me to conclude that their priorities were simply different, but not worse than mine.

That piece gives the reader a vivid picture of the writer, and Georgetown, Kenyon, Denison, and Dickinson thought so too.

Other favorite topics that are deadly without some specific message: cutesy lists of things the essayist likes are hackneyed topics that arouse reader hostility, as do stories of successes, athletic or other; the death of a pet; autobiographies ("My name is . . ." or "Hello, I'm . . ."); statements of the writer's sterling qualities; and pontifications on one of the world's pressing issues.

In this account of one small athletic success, the writer makes an illuminating point about himself. He shows you— just as *The Elements of Style* says to—how winning one tennis match made him see how he was falling short. See how much more enlightening and engaging it is than some musty generality like, "Through winning I learned the virtue of self-discipline."

In my first tournament, I really didn't strive to win and play to the best of my ability. My feeling was that I'd be content with losing to a player of higher caliber than I was. My goal was not to lose to an opponent of less ability than mine. If I did lose to a person ranked below me, my personal ranking would be in jeopardy. The next year, halfway into the same tournament, I realized I had a chance to win the championship. I had beaten an opponent in the quarterfinals who was ranked above me and the rest of the players were no better than I was. This was when I realized how inappropriate my goal had been. From that point on I knew that if I wanted to win, I couldn't be content with losing; a ten-dollar entrance fee was paid to win, not to be satisfied with losing. That kind of expectation would not allow me to reach my expectations in tennis or in life. The result was that I went clear to the finals. I lost, and for the first time, I felt discouraged after losing to a player of a higher caliber. I wasn't satisfied in the manner in which I had approached the tournament. With better preparation and more confidence in myself, I could have won the match. Never again would I be content with losing. From then on, my goal was to win, nothing less. My practicing became more strenuous and my concentration level rose to a new high. I learned to discipline myself while practicing. By taking full advantage of my abilities, my Maryland state ranking rose from number 26 one year to number 8 the next. This competitive spirit also applied to other aspects of my life. I was more motivated to complete my schoolwork and to participate more actively in extracurricular activities. Instead of being trite and unappealing, schoolwork became a challenge.

He was accepted at Rensselaer, Worcester Polytechnic, the University of Rochester, and Washington University, and is now a Defense Department engineer on a project in Asia.

A similarly effective vignette was written by the editor of a high school literary magazine, but his topic was people rather than prose because he found that:

> . . . after four months on the job I consider the honor to be less important than the actual experience . . . a valuable opportunity to deal with human nature. . . . Differences of opinion and personality caused my job to take a turn I had not expected. Section editors and their assistants became enemies. . . . Business managers complained of interference. . . . I took the sensitive approach to the problem. I began a campaign of asking, not telling, people to try and work together. . . . This, and several individual conferences, has resulted in a more comfortable situation for everyone. . . . There is a great difference between this experience and, for example, my experiences on athletic teams. In crew there is one leader, the coxswain, who asks for no opinions. . . . As an editor I have found it is necessary to ask opinions, to accept advice and to be sensitive. . . . Life is not as simple as a narrow boat concerned only with speeding in a single direction. It is more like an organization of many individuals with multiple directions and speeds, all of which must be considered in the administration of leadership.

The admissions people at Vassar were won over by this perceptive piece of self-awareness.

In Search of a Topic

This comes close to being the universal agony, but it can be solved sooner or later, as one girl found, by asking yourself enough questions and thinking about what's interesting or important to you. The following example is an ideal model because the writer picked a subject important to her and then proved her point with specific examples of how music helped her in many different kinds of situations. The Caramellos provide a happy, light touch:

> After trying to write this essay for several weeks, I realized that I'm having trouble because I express my deepest feelings, not through words, but through music. Whenever I'm upset, or bored, or frustrated, or happy, I play the piano or listen to music. When I'm feeling happy I go to the piano and bang out "Magnetic Rag" by Scott Joplin or Debussy's second "Arabesque." When I'm tired or depressed I play through some Chopin Nocturnes or Joplin's "Bethena." When a friend of mine unexpectedly killed himself last spring and I had to spend several hours home alone after hearing the news, I pounded into the piano Mozart's Sonata in A Minor, which he wrote about the death of his mother. Somehow it helped. Late that spring, when I got an "A" on my English term paper, I came home, turned volume up to ten, and danced around to Bruce Springsteen. When I miss my friends from music camp, I listen to "Spring" from Vivaldi's *The Four Seasons*, which a close friend played in several recitals. I also listen to Moussorgsky's *Pictures at an Exhibition*, which the camp orchestra performed at its last concert. My mother once

said that music is my emotional crutch. She could add chocolate and orange juice to that list. As I wandered around my house, looking for inspiration for this essay, I passed the boxes of chocolate bars that I'm selling to raise money for my school choir and barely resisted the temptation to demolish the Caramellos, thereby putting myself further in debt to the choir. I think I rely more on music than chocolate, however. At least it's not fattening. I started playing the piano when I was seven years old. I was eager to start because I had heard my mother and older sister playing for years. In fifth grade, my class staged *The Phantom Tollbooth* and I, after setting new words to use the song "Tomorrow," played while my friends sang. Three years later I found myself once again at the piano while my friends sang as I accompanied my junior high school choir. The next year I practiced my scales in a damp little cabin in the middle of Maine during my first summer at New England Music Camp. Every morning at camp I watched the mist rise from the lake, revealing white cottages surrounded by pines on the far shore. My days were filled with lessons, practice, and sports. I learned how to conduct; I learned how to sail; I learned how to clean toilets. And I concentrated on my music. Last summer I learned Beethoven's *Pathetique Sonata*. My favorite part about camp, however, was the people. They shared my love for music. I know this love will stay with me, whatever I do in life, to express my greatest joys and soothe my deepest disappointments.

Yale was lucky enough to get her, although others tried.

The Assigned Topic

Here the applicant had six inches of space in which to tell something about herself. She gave a one-two-three recitation of her interests and then hit a home run with her socko climax on her goals:

> My interests are varied. I like to draw, act, and ride. Most of my extracurricular activities involve drawing or acting. I am art editor of the literary magazine and of the yearbook, and I have played the leads in several plays, including *Taming of the Shrew*—but I have also managed the football and wrestling teams, and I am the movie critic for our two school newspapers. Last year I went to the Sidwell Friends School in Washington, D.C., on a school exchange program, and then I stayed over the summer in Virginia and worked as a riding teacher. Right now I am experimenting with myself; I am trying to find something I want to pursue in college and as a career. My problem, however, is that I like doing everything I have done. I love to draw; sometimes I want to be a famous artist and hang my paintings in the Metropolitan. But I also love to act, and sometimes I want to be a famous actress on Broadway. Sometimes I want to be president of IBM or of the United States. I want to be another Picasso, or Plato; I want to solve the world's peace problem and then discover the cure for cancer. My future plans are indefinite, but my goals are infinite. I want to do everything and be everything, and I want to be the best.

Facts that might be in the data part here illustrate the range of interests that tugged at her. From Johns Hopkins she went to Columbia as a Nicholson Fellow, working for a doctorate in English literature. A too-helpful parent might have tried to get her to cut the last sentence.

Here is another that makes its point on one page, in about three hundred words. The question was to describe some idea or intellectual experience that had an impact:

My encounter with the mathematical limit changed my life by expanding my narrow views. Before exposure to it, I viewed the world in extremes; black and white, or good and evil. When a limit was first explained to me, I was mystified; how could a number be found to render an infinite expression finite? In other subjects, such as English, I had learned that paradoxes existed; Charles Dickens wrote, "It was the best of times, it was the worst of times," but to me these were not insights into life, they were puzzles to tantalize the imagination and confuse the mind. The fact that mathematics, the field that I could always rely on to be logical, contained a paradox utterly confused me; yet this paradox eventually led to a deeper understanding of life. When, after many months of mental turmoil, my mind expanded to encompass this challenging idea, I began to view the world differently. If a numerical expression need not be finite or infinite, then why must an answer be correct or incorrect? Why must an action be good or bad? Why must people be intelligent or stupid? If parameters as strict as those bounding finite and the infinite can be

bent, ignored, and at times surpassed, then how can
terms as ambiguous as good, correct, and intelligent
be strictly defined? Once this theory crystallized in my
mind, I realized I had to change my perspective on life.
As John Keats states so lyrically, life is not absolute; it is
a glorious array of shades and intensities of all
colors. Through my exposure to the conceptual limit, a
new world was opened to me, a world without
theoretical limit.

Amherst, whose question that was, got her. The disappointed suitors were Williams, Carleton, and Middlebury.
Williams even offered her extra-early acceptance, although
she hadn't even applied for early acceptance, and the Amherst admissions director wrote that she enjoyed reading the
application. Who wouldn't?

Parental Help: The Great Peril

If an admissions officer suspects a student's statement is
not his own work, the almost certain reaction is rejection.
I know of one case when an A student suffered such a
fate. But short of that, parents often hurt by pressuring the
youth to play it safe, to avoid mention of a sticky or con-
troversial topic, or they try to impose their ideas of how a
topic should be handled. One father, for example, didn't
want his daughter to mention her work for the legalization
of marijuana, although it fit in with her pattern of activism,
not her habits. When she asked me, I told her to include it

and say why. If the college had objected, it wouldn't have been worth going to. Pointing out bad grammar or unsupported themes is all to the good; in short, the parent should function only as eagle-eyed critic, not as creator or coauthor. But no amount of warning is going to keep them from thinking that they can improve things, when what they usually do is censor all the spontaneity and life out of the essay.

The Very Personal Statement of the Underachiever or Child of Divorce

The person who hasn't performed anywhere near his ability has a chance to shrive himself when an application form asks, "What else would you like the admissions office to consider?" Or, he can append a statement telling why he hasn't done as well as he should. Divorce, for example, invariably affects a youth's performance if the breakup occurs around the age of puberty, and admissions officers are sensitive to this. Here is how one young man's honest confrontation with himself made believers of every admissions director who read it:

> What else would you like the Admissions Office to consider in evaluating your application? Perhaps there is *personal information that would help in interpreting your academic record* or in *understanding you as an individual.* Transfer students should use this space to explain why you wish to attend William and Mary.

Boarding the plane I smiled, seeing that I was doing the right thing; but I wasn't. I was running away from my problems as I always had.

My family had forced me to run to England to go to school. Problems at home were too great for me to handle and any attempt to put the pieces back together would be futile. I had tried ever so hard and my school report had shown my emotional beating. My grades had plummeted and I did not even try to pick them up for I "had better things to do" even though I never found out what they were. The only thing I picked up was a shell to crawl into.

The day I arrived in England was dark and rainy; I wondered what had happened to my bright and cheery sanctuary. That day was a harbinger for the ones to come. Only part way through the year all my problems seemed to catch up with me and new ones constantly developed. I struggled through the longest year and left as soon as I could, right after the final exams. England's fertile land did not help me grow. I ran back to America and into a prep school.

On registration day everyone greeted me with a saccharine smile and gave me a handshake filled with insincerity, but the sky was blue and the day was pleasant. I put my room together, and dusted my topmost shelf, and then only had four hours until dinner. That day I found out exactly how long four hours is. No year had been so painful; my grades stayed where they were, in mediocrity, no matter how hard I thought I worked; friendship seemed ever so scarce, and life seemed so fruitless. But, I did not run away at the end of the year.

I came back the next fall with even more problems weighing me down; but I decided that I was finished running away from problems and I started to confront them. At first, it was very painful and the results seemed slow in forthcoming. However, I first noticed that people began to accept me more and more as I crawled out of my shell. I began to form solid relationships and not ones based on insincerity. I began to want to work hard, not just think I was working hard, and my grades slowly began to reflect such a change in attitude. I took my first step in emotional growth.

I started to look at my problems with my family, and they seemed smaller, and much more manageable. I could talk to my father about my problems openly and also discuss his too. My mother's new family seemed so much less abrasive, and I could begin to accept them. I began to accept all problems, and understand that it was not just the problems at home that forced me away but some of the problems inside of me also. I saw that it was my fault too. I no longer needed a scapegoat. I no longer needed to run.

Yes, he was accepted by William and Mary as well as the others.

A Bad One and a Good One, from the Same Underachiever

The first statement was written in early spring of her senior year; the second after she had been working for a few months and had time to think things over. The first one:

For 7 years I attended———, a "magnet" school near my home. It seemed that the only attraction of this "magnet" was the TAG, or Talented and Gifted program. We students were rounded up and put in a room where we worked on long, laborious, and tedious projects and did "task cards"—problem-solving skills involved on an advanced level. I eventually dropped out of this program because it seemed to me that I hadn't been enriched a bit for it. Throughout my elementary school years I was placed in classrooms 2 or 3 grades above mine, and was ostracized for my abilities and my "weirdness." My grades were never top-notch. I believe this was because of the social needs, depression, and dissatisfaction with my environment. I attended———, a private Episcopalian preparatory institution, for 2 years after that. My grades improved greatly and I learned many things which still provoke my thoughts and interest, but I was extremely unhappy—both with the school and with my home life. Both the religious convictions of the school, its curriculum, and its staff, and the conservative, affluent condition of the student body contributed to my dissatisfaction. My parents had intended that I attend———through my graduation, but I felt my social life and mental health were being compromised in that environment; I enrolled at——— senior high as a TAG student. I believe that my previously inhibited and repressed feelings of individuality took control of my senses; I "acted out" my fantasies of being "wild" by skipping school, spiking my hair, and fighting constantly with my parents. Needless to say, my performance suffered greatly academically. This aberrance gradually diminished, and although my grades did not improve markedly, my attitude and manner became more contained; the recklessness of my freshman year dissipated into a strong penchant for fun and parties. I believe that my high school years have been, for the most part, debilitating to my intellect. The mediocrity with which I am surrounded is depressing, and academic excellence only accentuates the distance between the have and have-nots in this school. TECH and TAG students are loaded with pressure from teachers and principals, who seem to merely seek prominence from their students' performances, and are taught that the only important knowledge is that which helps one pass standardized tests. Obviously, this scene does not pique my interest and motivate me to seek academic excellence. Therefore, I take from my classes that information I know to be relevant and important to my life, and that is enough for me. I don't believe I'll ever memorize facts for the sheer purpose of passing a test—I need to *feel* that I am learning for a purpose. I am very inquisitive, alert, and informed, and I will not hesitate to question that which I find hard to swallow. I am nervously certain that I will be a vibrant and active member of a college community—the *right* college community, however, is still rather hazy to me now. In the future, I plan on realizing and achieving many personal goals. I will do this armed with knowledge, integrity, and a strong will. I intend to leave this life having made a definite and unmistakable mark by changing that which is wrong, helping those who are ignored, and never hesitating to stand up for what I believe in.

That statement would have made anyone question whether she could function in college when everyone was out of step with her, no matter how praiseworthy her values and goals. But when school ended, she got a telephone-answering job where she could see some of the legislative process in operation, and some of her school dissatisfactions seemed smaller. Also, at that age, change comes faster than at any other time in life. After a few months, she wrote this one:

> For the majority of my school years I agonized and fought against a system I felt was too impersonal and competitive, and I made things very hard for myself. I'm sure I confused most of my teachers by displaying high ability and low performance. I simply did not care for their methods of teaching and their lack of motivation. The competitive attitude of my fellow students intimidated me and I responded by displaying a lackadaisical, devil-may-care outlook on scholarly endeavors. If only I could find the right atmosphere, I thought and still do think, I would revive and perform to my ability. I have changed dramatically in my tastes and interests just in the last four years. Where once I found hard-core music and alarming clothes and hairstyles desirable, I now lean towards more mellow music and a less violent lifestyle. The anger I once felt toward the Establishment (embodied in the school system) has dissipated and been replaced with a yearning to see things change for the better so that today's children will have a more altruistic and caring environment and attitude in their school experience. The most important ingredient in

any education, in my opinion, is a motivation to learn in order to help humankind . . . not make lots of money. While very few people of my age are certain of what they want their future to hold, I am gradually learning what I *don't* want—for instance, I definitely do not want to be employed in the food service business. I do not want to perform manual labor. I do not enjoy computers and mathematics, and while I love science in all its branches, the formulas and haze of numbers surrounding it frighten me a bit. On the other hand, I am beginning to learn more about what I want to do. Politics fascinate me, and working on Capitol Hill this summer has given me great insight into the give-and-take personal politicking of our nation's Senate. While I have seen that much time is wasted on trivial matters such as quorums and the like while important bills on aid to the homeless wait, I think I am beginning to understand how things are done. It is frustrating, and this fascinates me even more. I have become active in the past six months regarding issues I feel are important. I have attended protests and done volunteer work for a few organizations and met many interesting and revolutionary people, and this has ignited the activist in me. I now have an outlet for my frustrations with the Establishment (now embodied in the government!) and I finally am doing something constructive with it. I never was interested in the "extracurricular activities" that seem so important to colleges these days. I preferred listening to twenty-year-old music and writing poetry to cheering at football games. I preferred reading books to joining the Math Club. I found the whole high school scene to be superficial and, frankly, useless in the great scheme of things. My attitude was, how can these people scream for a football team while nuclear war threatens our planet? This is extremist, I realize, and I probably missed some fun times. But I am glad I am this way. I believe the world needs more extremists, or the people cheering for the football team will never find out about acid rain and AIDS and homelessness. Well, that's the thumbnail sketch. Suffice it to say that I am different from my peers in many ways, and I intend to make lasting contributions in my lifetime to the betterment of my descendants.

It should not surprise you to learn that this courageous young lady, willing to let her essays be used in the hope of helping others, started with a bang at Antioch and is now a New York University Law School alumna with a straight-A record, and a good lawyer.

The Future Rewards of Doing a Good Job

You are not likely to think of the college application as anything more than a onetime chore. Wrong. It's a useful start on shaping yourself up for the job-hunting process after college. Today the application process is the most important aspect of job hunting. Employers are far more interested in a prospect's ability to think and to think clearly as evidenced by his ability to write and to speak well and how he works with others than they are in his grades, his major, or the name of the school he went to. As reported elsewhere in this book, several college investigating teams found that these were the qualities on which all kinds of employers, government and private, base their decisions. The agony and sweat invested now will help produce a better résumé and a better interview four years hence; you've had some very valuable practice, and that practice will pay off.

CHAPTER 15

The Interview? Relax!

THE SWEATY PALMS, THE TENSENESS, and the surging adrenaline are seldom necessary. Like the choice of major, the interview is one of the most overrated concerns in this whole college business. The number of colleges that require interviews is small, for a very good reason: unless it is an unusual case, the interview is seldom going to reveal anything the admissions office doesn't already know from the application data and the recommendations. There are very few surprises.

To anxious teenagers it is probably impossible to overemphasize this point: the chances of an interview being the make-or-break element approach zero. What it is most likely to do is to confirm or lend support to the other evidence. Except for the rare case when it can provide needed additional evidence, it is, like the vermiform appendix, pretty much the vestigial remnant of another time, of little value in and a negligible influence on most admissions decisions. Nevertheless, admissions offices are daily filled with hopefuls expecting their interviews to make points toward acceptance. For the most part, they could spend the time more productively working on good application statements.

The person who most needs a good interview is hardly ever the one hoping to make brownie points; she is the one needing to explain something in her past, how a parental divorce, for example, or an illness or her own adolescent attitudes affected her performance. These are some of the situations where an interview could—by filling in a missing part of the picture—make or break an admissions decision. But that has to be said guardedly, for a good interview could hardly overcome a bad application. What the applicant writes about himself is there in permanent black and white, where every member of the admissions committee, not just the person who interviews him, can see it.

While most colleges still grant interviews, of the eight Ivies and three Little Ivies, for example, only Harvard requires one, and it refers the applicant to a local alumnus. Some don't even mention interview in their admissions procedures. Many would abolish them entirely if they weren't afraid they'd be accused of a lack of interest, especially when the competition is giving them. Just stop to think: when a college is swamped with over five thousand applications, as Amherst and several others are, or eighteen thousand, as the universities of Michigan and Virginia are, no admissions staff, even with student help, could possibly interview more than a fraction. Most public institutions don't bother. In Virginia's case, only about two thousand are interviewed, so in fairness to the other sixteen thousand, no interview notes go into the applicants' files. Nevertheless, high school seniors flock to Charlottesville for the empty rite of a group session and tour.

Forty and fifty years ago, with a smaller population, the most selective colleges could offer interviews to most of the candidates, and many required them. Now they tend to make a difference only in the marginal cases or those where some unusual circumstances, perhaps beyond the candidate's control, have affected his record. For the vast majority of colleges, an interview is simply not necessary. A good college that takes much over half of its applicants is going to take any and all who have good records and who write acceptable applications. Indeed, I tell most of my clients to forget about an interview when they visit a college and get on with the sampling and testing of the merchandise to find out whether it's right for them.

I do urge clients to seek interviews if they are marginal, if there's been a problem somewhere in the background and the admissions director would like to see the candidate himself, or if the college requires one. Otherwise, what new evidence is the college going to discover about this person? His academic record, his activities, what his teachers and perhaps an employer think about him, are all on the record. What he has written about himself demonstrates how well he can think and express himself. With all that evidence in hand, it's going to be a rare candidate who surprises, or adds anything that changes the picture. However, many years ago, much to my surprise, a client with a 2.6 grade point average got into a grade-A New England college partly because he interviewed as well as he wrote.

What Is a Good Interview?

A good interview is a good conversation. It is not an occasion for reviewing your résumé, and certainly not for posturing, bragging, or faking. A good discussion means both parties are active contributors, that there's an exchange of ideas, that it's lively, that it ought to have some spontaneity and fun, that it can move easily from topic to topic and is not self-conscious. It may have nothing to do with the weighty business of college; it may be about baseball or reading or your or the interviewer's favorite topic. The candidate's poise or charm doesn't count. It's not the hairdo but what's under it.

How Does One Prepare?

The best preparation is one that enables you to come into the interview with an understanding of yourself and what you want out of college and out of life. If you know yourself, you are talking from strength. Why? Because you are ready to respond to questions about yourself as if you knew what you were talking about. Further, you will be able to take conversational initiatives instead of merely reacting. Such self-knowledge is not a condition most teenagers find themselves in naturally. To achieve some measure of it, do the questioning of yourself suggested in the chapter on why you want to go to college; then you can meet the interviewer on even terms.

What Kinds of Questions Do They Ask?

Even if it's just as a courtesy, one is likely to be, "Do you have any questions?" You ought to have at least one that's of genuine interest to you, and one that will make your interviewer sit up and take notice. Some of mine would be: Are students here learning for the sake of learning or for grades? To what extent are the students involved in their own education, or are they largely lecture-listeners? What will this college do for me? Do students form friendships with faculty members? But don't ask questions that reveal you haven't done your homework, i.e., that you haven't looked at the catalog or the student guide they may have sent you.

The odds are they will ask what your interest is in their school, what you've done outside the classroom, what you've done with your summers, perhaps what you've read recently, or if you have some great interest.

Some interviewers are students, some professionals, some are good and some are not; if you've done your homework on yourself, you'll do very well.

An interview with an alumnus affords an opportunity to question one of the institution's products. It can supplement a college visit; he is some of the merchandise you can test. Look over the questions in the chapter on visits. What did the school do for him? Would the alum send his own child there? If he had it to do over, would that college still be his choice? And so on.

Some Obvious Commonsense Tips

The only important thing about dress and hair is that they be neat.

You should look your interviewer in the eye, use his name, be positive, and be a lively conversational partner; but think—don't go off half-cocked. And no limp handshake!

Have a copy of your high school record with you.

It goes without saying that honesty is not just the best policy; it is the only policy. Ditto for exaggeration, puffery, or poor manners; that way lies disaster.

As Dr. Faustus explained to his apprentice eager to have the secret: "Be honest if you would be eloquent."

CHAPTER 16

Some Truths about Financial Aid

BE WARY OF THE MODERN SELLERS of wooden nutmegs.

The big scam artist of colonial days was the Yankee peddler selling wooden nutmegs. Today, soaring college costs have created an industry poised to take advantage of anxious parents and students facing one of the largest investments of their lives. Key in the words "financial aid for college" on any Internet search engine, and you will find almost 20 million matches. Therefore, your first source of information and assistance should be the colleges and their financial aid offices.

Here are the main points to consider:

1. You're not going to endanger your chances of admission by applying for aid unless you are in the bottom 1 percent or so of that college's pool, and you also need a great deal of aid.

The standard of good practice historically has been to keep decisions on admission and financial aid separate, a policy called need-blind admission; in other words, whether a candidate had applied for aid had no effect on the decision to admit or deny. But in the early 1990s three forces tended to make some schools at least need-conscious: the increasing costs of college, more intensive bidding for top students draining aid funds, and the Justice Department's antitrust action against a group of prestigious colleges for making uniform aid offers.

While the bidding for students helps the consumer, especially those at the top of their classes or minorities, many colleges either have barely enough aid money to go around or are running deficits in their aid budgets. What this means is that students in the bottom 1 percent are in danger of rejection if they have high need and the college is not need-blind. Some colleges admit them and deny aid. It also means that the college may meet only 80 or 90 percent of some applicants' needs.

With the present demographic trend, the "baby boom echo" winding its way through high schools and not expected to decrease until 2009, the bottom 10, 15, or even 20 percent who need a lot of aid may be in danger of receiving little or no financial help. They can protect themselves by calling the financial aid office and asking bluntly what the score is. They should get courteous treatment and a helpful answer. If not, they should by all means e-mail, write, or call and tell the college president.

Many colleges offer different kinds of aid packages for identical needs depending on how badly they want an applicant, by juggling the proportion of grant to loan and job.

Depending on the mission of the college and the goals for enrollment each year, a student matching these criteria might expect to see the aid offer enhanced.

In any case, if the college admits you—which means it wants you—it is going to do its best to give you all the aid for which you qualify. If you show that you deserve more, the school no doubt will make an adjustment and give you more grant and less self-help, or more overall. Remember that responsibility for paying for college starts with the family, and financial aid is meant to be the bridge that allows access—not the sole means of getting there. As John Urish, financial aid officer at Beloit College, points out, "Aid officers and colleges are there to distribute finite resources in a fair way that may make attaining an education that would otherwise be unaffordable, a possibility."

No parent should just sit and fret about what the college's attitude might be when the solution is so easy: just call and ask, or start by visiting the college financial aid Web site. Many college financial aid Web sites will post a breakdown of their aid packages by family income or, like Beloit College, offer a process for an early estimate of aid. Don't wait until the last minute to ask, and be ready to supply financial information in order to get an informed response. The financial aid officer will tell you, and he is honor-bound to tell you frankly what the school's policy is and how it might affect your child. That's his job.

I've often had to assure parents that they are not putting themselves at risk by asking how to complete the aid form. The important thing to remember is that if one college says no, there are several others every bit as good that will be glad to say yes if you give them a chance and approach them in a respectful manner.

2. Don't be afraid to apply for aid, even if your income is in the $100,000 range and you have two children.

The average income of families who get aid has been rising along with inflation. For example, in 2006, of all the families who received aid at Beloit College, those with family income of less than $40,000 averaged grant support in excess of $25,000. However, those receiving aid with incomes above $100,000 averaged about $12,000 in aid. According to John Urish, in many cases those resources came in the form of scholarships, but there are more than a handful who truly qualified for need-based grant support due to other circumstances, including the number of family members, age of parents, and other details that might not be apparent at first glance from the Free Application for Federal Student Aid (FAFSA).

Parents sometimes ask it if would be smart to not ask for aid until the sophomore year. The answer is no. It looks manipulative, with the exception of families where circumstances have dramatically changed. Aid directors are smart and savvy, and you are taking an unnecessary risk of running into a college with a severely capped aid budget. You want the financial aid officer to be a partner in the process, not an adversary, and starting off on the right foot goes a long way in the end.

3. Don't waste your money on a financial aid adviser or scholarship locator. Neither one of these fast bucksters can get you anything the college admission and financial aid staff won't give you free.

Today, with college costs soaring, there are two groups waiting to take your money: the consultant eager to help you apply for financial aid and the scholarship locator. One holds out the hope of beating the system, the other of pie in the sky. Don't waste your money on either; you may get not only stung, but hurt. If you have to pay to get money, it is probably a scam. Every year, several hundred thousand students and parents are defrauded by scholarship scams. The victims of these scams lose more than $100 million annually. Scam operators often imitate legitimate government agencies, grant-giving foundations, education lenders, and scholarship matching services, using official-sounding names containing words like *National*, *Federal*, *Foundation*, or *Administration*.

The Scholarship Fraud Prevention Act of 2000 was enacted to enhance protections against fraud in the offering of financial assistance for college education. It does so by three measures: increasing the penalties for people who perpetrate scholarship scams; eliminating a loophole in bankruptcy law that allowed the scam artists to retain their ill-gotten gains by exploiting the homestead exemption; and requiring the U.S. Department of Education, in cooperation with the Federal Trade Commission, to publish information about scholarship scams on its Web site.

So if anyone claims that for $250 he can get you $1,000 or $5,000, report that con artist to the authorities. If you are reading this too late and your money is gone with no gain, reporting the hustler may result in jail time because of the new provisions in the act.

Every year parents read or hear the myth that there are hundreds of millions of dollars in scholarship money going unused. It is a myth—but people cling to the hope. As many a financial aid officer has pointed out, if it's not being used, it's because it can't be used. The resources mentioned at the end of this chapter will lead you to Web sites that allow you to read for yourself the criteria required to apply for many small scholarships offered through local and national organizations. The sums are small compared to the cost of tuition, room, and board, but they might pay for a semester's worth of books.

It is the college financial aid officers who are either the source of or the conduit for 95 percent of the $134 billion of aid given. Furthermore, they are the individuals making the critical decision about your aid application and package. Get to know them, since they are invested in enrolling and keeping you at their college.

Since the first edition of this book in 1990, merit or non-need-based scholarships have become part of the landscape of college admissions. They are used to attract students of high ability who might not otherwise consider some of the lesser known but excellent liberal arts colleges. A dramatic example is provided by Wabash, the first-rate men's college in Indiana. Thanks to Eli Lilly, it is far and away the richest fount of such wealth proportional to size in the country. Over 80 percent of its eight-hundred-plus students get no-need merit scholarships averaging over $10,700 a year.

No-need merit awards range from those so tough as to be discouraging to the many simply requiring an additional interview with faculty and admission committees to determine interest and fit with the college. What many colleges look for is not just straight-A averages and perfect test scores but students who have other interests and talents to bring to the college community.

Many students, and even more parents, ask about pitting one college's aid package against another as a means of negotiating more money. It comes down to good manners: asking for a clear explanation of one financial aid versus another is acceptable, and once again, the financial aid and admission officers want to be helpful and honest, even if the answer is "no" to an increase in the package.

But if a family considers shopping around to save a thousand dollars or so, it must decide whether a smaller cost today is as important as the educational experience's lifelong effect. As with most things, the original cost is soon forgotten when the purchase gives satisfaction.

4. Inform yourself. The electronic world provides easy access to financial aid information at the touch of a keypad, and it's *free!* Your guidance office can also assist with the process, and if you prefer a publication to the Internet, they usually have hard copies of resources like *The College Cost Book*, published by the College Board.

The following links will provide information on how, where, and when to apply for aid:

- www.fafsa.ed.gov   The Department of Education's Web site, where you can find the Free Application for Federal Student Aid.
- www.collegeboard.com   College Scholarship Service (CSS) profile location.

- www.fastweb.com   A comprehensive resource for scholarship research.
- www.finaid.org   The "Smart Student's Guide to Financial Aid" and calculator.
- www.SallieMae.com   General resource information about the financial aid process.
- www.WinScholarships.com   Scholarship search site.
- www.SuperCollege.com   Another scholarship search site.
- www.studentaid.ed.gov/guide   *Funding Education Beyond High School: A Guide to Federal Student Aid 2007–8*, the Department of Education's comprehensive resource on student financial aid.

These sites provide detailed information on the process of applying for financial aid and list frequently asked questions. The finaid.org site enables parents to calculate what they're likely to have to contribute to college costs. It is wise to do this early and be informed, rather than assuming that you will or will not qualify for aid. Every year financial officers tell the tales of families who mistakenly fail to apply for aid because "someone told me I wouldn't qualify" and then miss out on funds that would have helped them pay the bill. Don't be misled by the advice of a well-meaning relative or neighbor. Go online, use the financial aid calculator and find out for yourself what your expected family contribution (EFC) will be. If you don't qualify the first year, it is still wise to apply the following year. If family circumstances change, such as a second child enrolling in college or a change in income, you may qualify for aid.

If you have questions, even early in the process, call the

financial aid officer at one of the prospective colleges on your list. They are there to help, and your interaction with them should be part of the research you do to determine if you want to attend.

5. Know how to apply for aid. Financial aid packages are part grant, part loan, and part campus job. How much of each depends on the family's need, the college's resources, and how badly the college wants you. The greater the need, the larger the grant is likely to be. The size of the grant may also be affected by how much money the college has in scholarship and loan funds, and whether the student qualifies for merit scholarships. Grant money from federal funds is given on a need basis, which is determined by applying federal methodology for need, set by Congress when reviewing the information on the financial aid form.

To apply for student financial aid from the federal government, including the Pell Grant, Perkins Loan, Stafford Loan, and work-study, you will need to submit the Free Application for Federal Student Aid (FAFSA). There is no charge for submitting this form. The FAFSA is also required by all state and many school student assistance programs. Applying online has the benefit of prompting you to provide missing information and identifying potential errors, so that the application you submit will be complete. You should apply as soon after January 1 as possible, once you have gathered the necessary financial information, but check with colleges for their deadline dates. Do apply for a FAFSA personal identification number (PIN), as you will need this to access and file your form.

Some private colleges and universities will require one or more supplemental forms to obtain information not included on the FAFSA. They may have their own forms, or they may ask you to complete the College Board's CSS Profile form. It is important to check the college Web site and read the information they provide, or call the financial aid office to find out which forms they require and what deadlines you will need to meet. Copies of the results are sent to the colleges the family has indicated and to the family for corrections, if needed. Deadlines are important when dealing with the distribution of funds. Miss a deadline, and the funds may be gone. The early bird gets the worm in this process.

Financial aid officers use both federal and institutional methodology to arrive at an expected family contribution (EFC), based on assets, income, number of children, and any unusual circumstances. The theory is that this is what a family should be contributing to that child's support, whether at home or at school. What these figures show determines eligibility for federal and state grants and some loans. The college's financial aid officer determines how much aid the family gets and how it is apportioned among grant, loan, and campus job.

6. Get to know the specifics of the various available loans and grants.

If family income is low enough to qualify, usually under $30,000, the student can get a Pell Grant. For 2006 the maximum awarded was $4,000. Someone eligible for a Pell Grant may also qualify for a Federal Supplemental Educational Opportunity Grant (FSEOG) if there's exceptional need. The maximum FSEOG is $4,050.

Also for students with exceptional need are the federal Perkins Loans. These are low-interest loans (5 percent), and students may borrow up to $4,000 a year, with a maximum of $20,000.

Everyone, whether he demonstrates need or not, is eligible for low-interest Stafford Loans. For those who demonstrate need, which would include Pell and FSEOG grant recipients, the interest is paid by the government while they are in college. For those who don't qualify on a need basis, interest accrues while they're in school. The interest rate is variable, and is set each June. In 2006 it was 5.3 percent. The borrower also pays an origination fee of 4 percent and usually an insurance fee of 1 percent. A freshman may borrow $3,500, a sophomore $5,500, and a junior and senior $5,500 a year.

For families who don't demonstrate need, but whose credit is good, there are PLUS loans whose limit is the cost of education, and whose interest rate is variable, but not higher than 9 percent. For those loans there's an origination fee of 4 percent and insurance premium of 1 percent.

But the best news, and the best deal for families who don't demonstrate need, is the direct loan program in which Congress authorized the Department of Education to make loans to students directly, cutting out all the expenses of middlemen and the difficulty of finding lenders. This means that both the Stafford and the PLUS loans can be negotiated directly with the Department of Education, rather than a bank or a credit union. An origination fee of 4 percent is charged.

The third part of the aid package is Federal Work Study, a campus job. The jobs pay minimum wage, and there is a limit on the number of hours, set by the college—usually ten to fifteen—on the theory that college ought to be a full-time endeavor.

Even if you don't qualify for aid, a campus or town job—which the student seeks after he arrives at school—can reduce the cost and provide spending money, besides providing the important function of letting a student work for part of her own education.

Finally, remember, the financial aid officers want to see you attend if you are admitted, and therefore they want to make it easier for you, if they can. Whatever you think your chances are, do apply for aid. Like the lottery, you've gotta play to win. You'll never know if you don't ask.

CHAPTER 17

If You've Made a Mistake, You Can Save Yourself

NO MATTER WHAT YOUR MISTAKE, you can correct it. Some mistakes can be shaken off without missing a beat; some may take a semester, and some two semesters. The very worst ones might take longer. But no matter what it is, you have plenty of company; lots of others have made the same mistake and gotten back on the right track. Countless thousands get into the wrong school every year, and every college, except the most selective, does a brisk business in transfers. But those very selective ones don't have a monopoly on either quality or desirability.

This message of hope applies across the board to:

- freshmen who wanted to take a year off but whose parents made them go to college anyway;

- freshmen who are frustrated or miserable in the wrong college;
- students who've found they're in a professional program they don't like;
- flunkouts;
- dropouts; and
- even students convicted of crimes.

The American college establishment is so big and so diverse that everyone can get a second and sometimes even a third chance. In no other country can a youth have so many different opportunities.

But because she doesn't know any better, and colleges sometimes misinform her, the student in the wrong pew or the erring one often thinks she can't improve her situation or save herself. She almost always can; religion isn't the only place where there's grace and redemption.

This doesn't necessarily apply to the person just looking for greener grass on the other side of the fence—the one who thinks a bigger, more urban place or more prestigious name would be better—nor to the one whose social life isn't what she thinks it ought to be (a principal, but usually temporary, cause of girls wanting to transfer). A freshman at Columbia, for example, who yearns to transfer to Harvard—or another equally selective school—might as well put it out of his mind. Illustrative was the experience of a Columbia freshman with a 3.6 average who wanted to transfer to Harvard, which had turned him down as a high school senior, despite an outstanding scholastic record and the editorship of the school paper to his credit. "All my life," he said, "I've been doing the things that Harvard wanted."

But it was to no avail; hordes of others had been doing the same thing.

The facts of life are that the most selective schools have so little attrition that the competition for what few transfer openings there are is two to five times greater than for freshman places. In fact, some—Dartmouth and Carleton, for example—don't even take transfers. A few years ago, after I had told the Oberlin admissions director about a prospect with two solid years of straight As who had outgrown her college, he said they'd be glad to "consider" her. I said, "You must not have heard me; she has two years of straight As." He said, "This year we've got at least three hundred applicants for twenty places, and I'd guess nearly half of them have straight As." But she did get in.

The Transfer Market for the Unhappy Student in Good Standing

As the Oberlin case indicates, the transfer market varies; in some years, when a lot of students were taking a year off, they would have come through the telephone after her. Since the 1990s, it has been more difficult to transfer into good, but not very selective, colleges than to get in as a freshman. Good colleges in the South and Midwest also have less attrition, but these two regions still contain most of the bargains, and this is where an unhappy student should find the quality and the ambience he's seeking.

Below a C Average? Don't Let Them Tell You There's No Hope

If an unhappy student has an average below a C, he may think he's stuck because a registrar or some other official has told him no other college will look at him. That just ain't so, but unfortunately, students often are told this and as a result don't try. There are always other options. If you're mired in engineering or some other professional program and hating it, or aren't making your grades because you just don't like the place, don't let anyone tell you that you can't get in anywhere else. You can. You don't have to be stuck with a bad marriage.

And that doesn't mean you'll have to take less or settle for Podunk. However, you may have to do penance of some sort. Often passing a couple of summer school courses or doing a term or a year's work will demonstrate the motivation the admissions office is looking for. Or, they may want you to raise your grade point average to a C overall. Then you'll have several suitable choices. Those tasks may take some extra time, but that's not the worst thing in the world, as we shall see a little further on.

The Student in College Against His Will

The youth whose parents made him go to college when he wanted to take a year off and who is failing should get out now and work a year or two until he's ready to go. As pointed out in chapter 1, staying in school under duress only

aggravates the problem. In thirty-five years as a college official or as a counselor, I have never known a kid to do well
when he's been pushed into going.

Even if such a student is not failing, his discontent is
more likely than not to breed trouble in the months ahead
in poor performance and the accompanying dissatisfaction.
It's likely to prove a waste of time and money as well. He's
better off getting out as soon as possible and doing something else while the maturing process does its work.

The Flunkout Can Rescue Himself

A typical example this summer was a youth who had been
academically suspended for a year by a school he heartily
disliked. He was happy to hear that three colleges said they'd
accept him, particularly because an official at his college had
told him that not only would no school take him, but that
he couldn't get credit for any work done in the suspension
year. He had spent the term after his dismissal proving himself by carrying a full course load at the local community college, making good grades, and holding a job besides. All
three colleges said they would give him credit for the community college work. The moral: since most college officials
know very little about the rules of most other institutions,
make your own inquiries. If anything, the kind of counseling
a student gets in college is often worse than that received in
high school, for this sort of case turns up year after year. And
there would undoubtedly be many more examples like this
if failing students refused to be brainwashed.

Even if this young man hadn't made the effort to prove he meant business, he would have had several options; there are always reputable colleges that need students. True, a student is not legal tender in the academic world if he doesn't have a C average or isn't eligible to return to his own college, but a lot of good admissions officers are willing to give him a second chance, particularly if he had a good high school record and there are extenuating circumstances, such as being in the wrong program or in a clearly unsuitable school. The latter happens most frequently when the parents have insisted on making the college choice, or on making the youth go when he didn't want to. An unscientific guess would be that half of all unhappy choices are the parents' fault.

I have always found plenty of admissions directors to be sympathetic when it seems obvious either that the student made a bad choice or that his parents pushed him into it, when he wanted to take a year off or go somewhere else. The student who makes the effort to change almost always winds up in a college he likes better and therefore profits from. It's useful to remember that admissions officers have common sense and are understanding. They're perfectly willing to bend or break the establishment's rules if there's a legitimate reason to do so, which usually means a reasonable expectation that the applicant will prosper with a change of scenery.

Sometimes the School Is Partly to Blame

When it seems clear a student's troubles may be all or partly the college's fault, an admissions director may finesse the rule that a student should be eligible to return to his original school. Several summers ago, for example, a young man came to me whose grades at Johns Hopkins had been going steadily downhill for three years, and he'd just been dismissed. He was a quiet, unassertive biology major unhappily caught in a mass-production, cutthroat premed competition. He was vaguely aware that his educational experience might be one-dimensional, but he had gotten no help or counseling from any adviser or teacher for three years. He had doubts about what he was doing and about himself. Invariably, anyone in trouble as a junior rings alarm bells, because it looks as if his pattern has been set. But this young man had made an outstanding high school record, or he wouldn't have met Hopkins's intense admissions competition in the sciences. Wooster's admissions office agreed that this fellow was a victim and in the wrong school, and admitted him for the fall term. He made the dean's list for three semesters at Wooster and went on to graduate school in another field.

The All-F Flunkout: A Rehabilitation Case

The person who flunks out just for lack of effort gets little sympathy. He's going to have to prove he means business. If he has failed his freshman year, he might do it with good grades in a community college for one semester. If he flunks out as a sophomore, the skepticism will be greater, and so will the demands on him. If it happens as a junior, he's in real trouble and might be well advised to stay out and work a year or two and get his priorities in order.

The Dropout from High School or College

The most dramatic example in my experience of how open the door is for high school dropouts was a client who had quit high school in the ninth grade, but who was a strong contender for a major fellowship as a college senior. After five years out of school, he took the General Educational Development test (GED), passed it, went to college, and was on the dean's list most of his time there. As chapter 1 points out, a high school diploma isn't needed to get into a good college.

The college dropout can always get back in if he's in good standing, but if he wants to return to the place he started, he'd be wise to make plans with the college before he leaves.

However, even if he never goes back, he can still have a rich, full life and do great things. One shining example I knew was Waller Barrett, who made a fortune by age forty-two and retired to become the celebrated bibliophile who gave his alma mater, the University of Virginia, its matchless collection of American literature, both first editions and original manuscripts. And he never got his degree.

The Student in the Wrong Program

A change of program may often mean a change of scenery. A dissatisfied student in architecture at Cornell, for example— as one young friend was—isn't likely to get into another Ivy League school or another department at his own school. That young man was in limbo, unable to transfer to the College of Arts and Sciences because he didn't have a C average in architecture: he was caught in the watertight compartmentalization of the university bureaucracy. But since he had a first-rate high school record, and it was obvious that he'd gotten himself into the wrong curriculum, he was able to get into a first-rate college that was much better.

Similarly, a creative youth who had the idea that engineering would be the perfect preparation for design found Georgia Tech to be a tough grind and an assembly line of huge classes where the teachers were either unavailable or foreigners barely able to speak English. He also found he didn't like engineering. He had only a 1.6 average at the end of his freshman year, but he took a couple of summer school courses to prove he was on track, and was able to get into a good college, one infinitely more likely to develop his creative instincts.

Another who chose engineering at Tulane, thinking that was the route to becoming a flier, found in his freshman year that he was not enamored of the field. In family conferences at the end of that year and midway into the next, puritan values prevailed, and it was decided that he should stick it out, although his interest, his morale, and his grades were all sagging. But like the fellow at Cornell, he couldn't transfer out to Arts and Sciences because he didn't have a C average. Since he'd had a good high school record, however, and it was clear his was a case of being in the wrong pew, three colleges said they'd take him. Two other good ones did after he got an A and a B in two summer school courses. So he wound up with his choice of three first-rate schools and two good ones.

The prospect of having to spend a semester or a year to be born again should not inspire dread reactions that your life is being truncated or somehow damaged. After all, the goal is to improve your situation and your long-term outlook. Teenagers nevertheless think the worst, and will continue to, because of a paradox of adolescence: a conviction of immortality cohabiting with a certainty they'll be over the hill by age twenty-one and that a whole year blocked out of that brief interim is just too much. A fine example of this teenager syndrome was exemplified in chapter 10 by the high school senior who said, "Well, anyway it's four years out of my life," but as a senior at Stanford was "aghast" to be told he'd said that.

Students Convicted of Crimes

I have had clients who have been convicted of various crimes, yet were accepted by and prospered in colleges; the question to be answered, naturally, is whether the person is now on track and seems likely to lead a law-abiding life. In one of many different kinds of cases, a college sophomore convicted of helping to steal two cases of wine intended for a faculty dinner got into another college. As is so often the case, the violation turned out to be a searing learning experience.

Two Important Things to Remember

In almost every case everywhere, grades go down as morale does. As a consequence, here are two vital injunctions to heed:

One, continue to work hard. If you decide to transfer, the better your grades are, the easier it will be. If your grade point average falls below the waterline C, your problem will be tougher.

Two, get out as soon as you can. Don't aggravate your troubles by sticking with a bad situation. As a former Oberlin dean said, "If you're on the wrong train, get off at the first stop."

CHAPTER 18

Should You Hire a Private Counselor?

If you can find a counselor who can expand your list of college choices and help you to plan your high school career or complete your college applications, yes.

But choose wisely; the woods are full of people who don't know what they're doing but make big claims. There is no legal certification; anyone can get into it, and it looks like easy money. Some work with a student all four high school years, charge fees of $30,000 or more, and guarantee acceptance at a desired school. Beware! For some schools, such an adviser would be the kiss of death.

In nearly forty years of counseling, I never got a client into an Ivy or Ivy clone, although several clients think I did. The clients got themselves in; I just helped them present themselves. Sometimes all it took was getting them to read *The Elements of Style* so they'd write better essays.

A professional group, the Independent Educational Counselors' Association, asks applicants for membership for their background and how many colleges they've visited in the last year. That's good—in fact, visits are the key—but the membership is still a mixed bag.

Such membership is nevertheless a far better credential than having been an admissions officer, which only means knowing something about a single college's rules and methods. Similarly, having been a high school counselor means nothing.

A good counselor is a knowledgeable adviser and advocate, presenting, defending, or sometimes pushing the student with the admissions officer. But that can go only so far. Unless the kid's family has given the school a lot of money, he's a legacy, or something special (see chapter 6), the admissions officer is going to make a professional decision, and what the applicant herself has done will speak far louder than any other voice. In fact, when it comes down to the wire, the applicant's is the only voice. The best that anyone can do is to help the student present herself to the best advantage. If she is a junior or rising senior, the most a counselor can do is to advise as solid an academic program as possible, and encourage involvement in outside activities.

By helping the student see what she wants to say in her application statements, a competent counselor can perform the function of a good editor or rhetoric instructor, helping her present herself as effectively as possible. In very competitive situations—as noted in chapter 14—this is crucial; it is where an applicant can set herself apart from all the others who have records as good or better.

But no ghostwriting. The adviser's job is to help the student see and be herself. Personal statements written by a hired hand won't work if the admissions office is on its toes. And as I note in chapter 14, many a meddling parent has hung his child. A student who has done a good job on her personal statements is also going to handle that vastly over-rated bugaboo, the interview, much more confidently and skillfully.

Many parents go to a private counselor for a very good reason: to seek out a range of intelligent choices in a day when the average private college costs over $30,000 a year, and schools (meaning you, the taxpayer and PTA member) don't make the costly effort to provide knowledgeable college advice by funding college visits.

The adviser's criteria should be much more than the client's grades, class rank, and test scores. He should know more about the college than their freshman profiles. He should be able to suggest places where a person interested in ideas, or in causes, or in things would fit. He should be able to suggest schools where students with learning disabilities have had successful experiences, not just consult directories. The mere fact that an institution has a program for the learning-disabled doesn't mean that its students pass their courses. A lot of lip service in scores of catalogs needs to be checked for truth in advertising.

The counselor's objective, in other words, is to try to make a match that will make a difference in the student's life. To be able to do this, he also has to know something about the child and her family: is it a happy or a broken home; does this kid live in the shadow of an achieving sibling or parent? And he has to get the child's confidence and trust. What hope does an overworked high school counselor have of doing this, especially when he may see a student only in glancing encounters, if at all, in four years?

What about Testing?

When a prospective client asks me if I do any aptitude or vocational testing, I say no—kids have been tested up one side and down the other for twelve school years, and unless it's a case for a psychiatrist, a psychologist, or a speech or reading therapist, the chances are that nothing very new or useful will be learned. If there is a learning disability, it *should* have been uncovered long before the student reached the eleventh grade. Similarly, even allowing for the natural abrasion between adolescents and parents, a personality problem should have revealed itself before then.

A desire for aptitude testing usually tells more about the parents than the student: they're worried because their child isn't getting good grades or doesn't know what career direction to be thinking about. (Neither did the parent at eighteen, after all.)

Such a test may be an interesting exercise, and it may relieve the parents, so if the family wants to spend money that way, fine; but it's not likely to affect the course of a teenager's life. When a family has had their child so tested, I always suggest waiting until after the interview to look at the test. Invariably, the interests or abilities elicited by the interview are the same ones the family has paid a fat fee to identify. More important is the thread that runs through this book: a teenager doesn't know what will engage him twenty years hence, and the things that will determine what kind of person he will be haven't happened to him yet.

Some Suggestions on Checking Out a Counselor

The first thing to do, obviously, is to ask for references and check out some of a counselor's former clients. Ask them if they'd send their own children to this person. If you can't get references, forget it!

Also, before spending a lot of money, call one or two of the colleges your child is interested in and ask the admissions officers if they have dealt with this counselor, whether they still will, and if not, why.

Ask the counselor where she went to college. This has a status-conscious smell, but it is relevant. If it was a rigorous, high-quality institution, that's a good sign. If it was a place mainly in the business of preparing teachers, whether big or small, that's a loud warning signal. Teacher-training institutions are vocationally oriented places of low standards, and hardly likely to acquaint anyone with a demanding intellectual experience. If it was a university, particularly one that's easy to get into, that's also a warning. Unless a counselor was in an honors program, she probably won't have had the benefit of being involved in her own eduction, of living in a community of shared values and expectations, or of a continuing dialogue with teachers.

Ask about professional background: How long has the counselor been doing this? And what was her preparation? Neither a degree in counseling nor years as a high school counselor is relevant. Undergraduate counseling courses are more shadow than substance, and no graduate course can impart common sense or intelligence, much less any real knowledge of colleges. As for high school counselors, when was the last time your school board budgeted funds for travel so guidance counselors could make workday visits to colleges? Unless school systems beef up their guidance staffs and balloon the budgets, the counselors can't do the essential homework.

One example of the consequent epidemic lack of suitable guidance is that of a girl with a 2.6 average at a selective girls' school whose school counselor recommended Cornell, Penn, Davidson, Duke, North Carolina State, and the University of Maryland. Considerations of suitability aside— and none were—she couldn't have gotten into any one of the first four, and the other two were safeties resulting from the counselor's ineptitude.

What *is* relevant is how many colleges the counselor has investigated, as described in chapter 11. Group tours don't count, whether conducted by the institution or not. Neither does a visit to talk to the sales staff in admissions. The question is, What can she tell you about the institution, its mores, the kind of people it produces, the atmosphere?

What Does the Counselor Claim to Do?

Is she saying she will get your child in college, smooth the path, help with applications, instruct for the interview, find the right school for your child's career interests? Is she saying she will match student and college? If so, how? What are her criteria?

If she advertises that "with our help" you can get into a "desired school, get grant and loan money," beware!

A competent counselor will help the student find a college that will help him grow, not one with a major that holds his adolescent interest. Those who start out with clear goals and never change their major are those least likely to graduate, several studies have found, while those who changed four times were most likely to finish.

So beware the counselor who promises to find an institution that has a very good program in just the specialty your child is interested in today. A competent counselor will help the student look at himself a little more clearly. A competent counselor will ask the kinds of questions that will elicit the student's values, goals, and interests and how he looks at himself in relation to the world, not whether he wants this or that program.

Ask the counselor how much reliance she places in the ratings of magazines such as *US News and World Report* or *Money*. These do much harm; the raters don't know the colleges, and their ratings are meaningless. They pretend to judge quality by quantifications, such as test scores, selectivity, and other data that miss the heart of the matter; they're pretentious, money-grubbing nonsense.

In short, a good counselor should have good rapport with and knowledge of the student and his family, and should be a person who inspires trust in her character and common sense and confidence in her knowledge. Just as you wouldn't choose a doctor who promised to cure you or a lawyer who assured you he'd win your case, beware the so-called counselor who makes such come-on claims.

CHAPTER 19

A Few Favorites

After decades of bragging, the Ivies have finally confessed they're failing at undergraduate education.

Two distinguished Ivy scholars, Dr. Stanley N. Katz of Princeton and Dr. Harry R. Lewis of Harvard, have both written exposés of the universities' sins in forgetting liberal education in the pursuit of excellence in research, as laid out in chapters 1 and 5. I asked Dr. Katz why he waited until 2005 to make his exposé. His reply was, "I'm discouraged; I just got around to it." He also commented that if he were going to college now, he'd go to a good liberal arts college.

A small-college scholar, Dr. Samuel Schuman, chancellor of the University of Minnesota's Morris campus, adds in his incisive and fascinating 2006 book *Old Main: Small Colleges in Twenty-first Century America*, "Some of us believe that the small campus undergraduate experience is not just valuable, but rightfully claims its place as the core collegiate unit, the sun around which the rest of the educational planets, even the giants, revolve." He also claims that these colleges "can be the very best places for stimulating creative and critical thinking, and where students come to know themselves."

And the period between seventeen and twenty-two is the time when kids come to know themselves. They can profit from graduate school at the universities when they're more mature.

Dr. Schuman made it plain, however, that the universities and small colleges are doing quite different jobs, and doing them for people of different age groups; one is not necessarily better than the other.

This chapter will confine itself to small colleges, not research universities or professional schools, such as art, business, drama, engineering, music, and so on. Also, this book looks beyond the Ivy League. (The one research university exception is Clark, which is also a small college that changes lives.) Because omniscience is in as short supply here as anywhere else, my list is nothing more than suggestions. It may induce you to include in your search colleges that you might have turned up your nose at.

Another important piece of advice on size: some people worry about a college being too small, but all the research that's been done on this topic indicates that the smaller college has more impact on the student and affects him more (in a good way) than a larger college, just as a class of a dozen is going to be more personal than one of four or five dozen.

In pushing the liberal arts approach, I could quote the English philosopher John Stuart Mill: "A man is a man before he is a philosopher, a physician or a carpenter and if you make him a reasonable and sensible man, he will make himself a reasonable and sensible philosopher, physician or carpenter." Yale said much the same thing at about the same time (long before it became a research institute) when it announced in 1828 that it would offer no professional or vocational courses, only theory and the liberal arts. A youth could specialize later.

High school seniors are seldom ready for the competition they will face in the vocational art or drama schools. But whatever their goals, in today's fast-changing economy, they need the four years of college to find themselves and get an education.

Colleges for a Wide Range of Abilities

The following colleges have track records in helping kids find themselves and producing moral adults, the often-forgotten job of college. It is also the recipe for making winners. These are places where you don't have to be an A student to get a better education and have a far better experience, inside and outside the classroom, than at the Ivies or their famous clones. They are inclusive, not exclusive, and they attract strikingly different kinds of kids. They range from the most intellectual and demanding colleges in the country (Marlboro, New, St. John's, and Reed) to St. Andrews Presbyterian.

In between are schools for the risk takers and those who march to a different drummer. All are profiled in the companion book to this one, *Colleges That Change Lives*. After each profile is a Ten Years Later section in which students testify to the college's lasting impact.

■ AGNES SCOTT, in an Atlanta suburb, has a long history of producing scholars, scientists, contributors, and other achievers. Students here think they have it a lot better than girls at a coed college: no boring males dominating class discussions, but plenty of males for a good social life at nearby colleges. They also have a lovely campus and Atlanta's Federal Reserve Bank, the Centers for Disease Control, and the city's famous art gallery as teaching resources.

■ ALLEGHENY has a long history of changing the lives of students with a wide range of abilities. It has long been a leading producer of future PhDs as well as CEOs. Among its attractions, and worth a detour, is a dream science building that the science faculty helped design. Along with Hendrix and Whitman, it is one of the three best sportsmen's paradises, offering equipment and lessons, in the college world.

■ AUSTIN, in Sherman, Texas, is a community of high standards that is now much more diversified; its lovely campus has about twice as many buildings as when I first visited it in the early 1990s.

■ BELOIT, ninety miles from Chicago in Wisconsin, is a wonderful school of great diversity, a happy, familial community that produces leaders in many fields. On my second visit in the early 1990s, I was having trouble finding students who had any gripes. In mid-afternoon, a boy snuck up to me and said in a low voice, "I understand you're looking for bad things about Beloit." It turned out he didn't like his political science prof.

■ BIRMINGHAM-SOUTHERN, in that Alabama city, would be outstanding in any company and is one of the gems of the South, thanks to the vigor and vision of former president Neal Berte and his successor, Daniel Pollick. Every student I talked to was enthusiastic—blacks, foreigners, and whites. Their athletes get better grades than the other students. It is a great school, and they'd like to have more northerners and westerners to augment their growing diversity.

■ CENTRE, in Danville, Kentucky, has long been *the* college for state residents. As one professor said, its students represent the corporate class of Kentucky. For them the choice has always been an Ivy school or Centre. It is so good that it is not unusual for children of faculty or administrators to start at some prestige college but transfer to Centre for their sophomore year in spite of having a parent so close. The children are right. And other children would like it; Centre wants more students from other regions. Its ancient trees and Federal architecture make a charming campus. Now 80 percent of the students have a foreign study term, and for good reason: the college "guarantees it" at no extra cost. Faculty members say they come back "transformed."

■ CLARK in Worcester, Massachusetts, is the only quality bargain in the Northeast, in that it is the only grade-A research university that has the spirit of a good small college, with the same kind of concern for the B student, which two deans said they preferred, for the excitement they get when he blossoms.

■ CORNELL COLLEGE in pretty Mount Vernon, Iowa, two hundred miles west of Chicago, has a lovely 129-acre campus with a lake, a fitting background for a beautiful campus with a new (in 2006) pedestrian mall that ties it all together. Its Life Sports Center is not only state-of-the-art, but breathtaking in its size and inclusiveness. Cornell is one of two colleges (Colorado College is the other) on the block system—one course at a time. Faculty as well as students love both the system and the school, and so would you. It is the only entire campus to be included in the National Register of Historic Places. In my book there is no better college, and it produces much more than its share of writers, scholars, and executives.

■ DENISON, in Granville, Ohio, has a long history of producing achievers, a beautiful campus, and a beautiful new life, thanks to a former long-term president, Dr. Tolela Myers, who changed it from a fraternity-dominated fallback school for easterners to one that transforms teenagers. Her successor, Dr. Dale T. Knobel, shares her vision. When I was there in the late 1980s, the student parking lot had a lot of Jaguars and BMWs and the black students, largely from the inner city, felt alienated and bitter. I didn't talk to a single one who had a good word to say for the school. Ten years later, the black students couldn't find enough affectionate words, and the fraternities no longer dominated, or even mattered much.

■ EARLHAM, in Richmond, Indiana, is another college than which there is no better. It is a Quaker school, but you'd never know it except that it's warm and caring and a community of consensus and the Golden Rule. Its eight-hundred-acre campus has six hundred acres devoted to horses, stables, and other things equestrian, as well as a rich biological resource and trails for jogging or horseback riding. Half of Earlham's students are children of educators and the college claims, from anecdotal evidence, that it has more Ivy League sons and daughters than any other college.

■ ECKERD in St. Petersburg, Florida, like the others in this group, is one that evokes superlatives. When it was only thirty-five years old, I wrote that Eckerd was a hot growth stock, it was such an attractive community of learning. It has exceeded my predictions. Its graduates think there's no other college so good.

■ EMORY & HENRY, in beautiful southwest Virginia's rolling hills, does a far better job of producing good citizens and contributors than any of the three prestigious schools in the state: the University of Virginia, William and Mary, or Washington and Lee. It is an extended family that uncovers unrealized talents, instills values, and develops the desire and ability to serve.

■ EVERGREEN STATE, on one thousand acres of towering evergreen forest six miles outside Olympia, Washington, is the most unusual public institution anywhere and, along with Reed and Whitman, one of the three best colleges in the

Northwest. It is a relaxed and informal community that works hard. I'm pretty sure I was the only one on campus who was wearing a jacket and tie, not to mention polished shoes. An indication of its diversity and tolerance is in the student union; it has offices for the gay and lesbian organization. A professor said to me, "We came here committed to making a difference."

■ GOUCHER, in Towson, Maryland, is one of the few colleges in a major urban area, on a lovely tree-lined 287-acre campus just outside Baltimore. Goucher thinks foreign study is so important that it has reworked its calendar to include two three-week terms in January and May so that whatever the major, a student can get in at least one foreign term. Close by the campus is Loch Haven Reservoir, a mecca for boaters and fishermen.

■ GUILFORD, a Quaker school in Greensboro, North Carolina, is the country's hottest producer of oil geologists. It has also been tops in the state in winning prestigious Danforth Scholarships. It is a warm and caring place. When I asked about various graduation rates, the answer was, "While I haven't bothered to look, blacks do as well here as whites and graduate at the same rate, 70 percent." Students are doing much research with faculty, and one of their successes has been a discovery that makes metal-free batteries for use in pacemakers possible.

■ HAMPSHIRE, in Amherst, Massachusetts, is a dramatic success story. It graduated its first class in 1970 but is already one of the top colleges in producing future scholars, movie makers, and winners in many fields. Ken Burns is an alum-

nus. It is in an active consortium with Smith, Mount Holyoke, Amherst, and the University of Massachusetts, and eight
to ten thousand students take classes at other campuses each
semester. But one Hampshire student told me, "We're the
only ones who talk about our work on the five-college
buses."

■ HENDRIX, in Conway, Arkansas, is absolutely lovely, an
underappreciated academic gem. It is also a sportsman's
paradise, with the Ozarks so close by. Its beautiful campus
goes well with its wonderful sense of community, a lot of
new buildings, and a new learning plan called The Journey.
Seniors have won scads more prestigious fellowships—
Watson, Goldwater, and Rhodes—than any other school in
the state. One of every eight doctors in Arkansas is a Hendrix
alum. A former president, Ann Dye, wanted to increase the
feeling of community and directed that the Christmas dinner be catered so the staff could attend. But the staff thought
they could do a better job, so they do it now.

■ HIRAM, in a lovely Ohio village of the same name, is a
national asset, a much underappreciated one. No college,
and certainly no university, works the same magic on young
minds and souls that Hiram does, or makes them meet
stiffer challenges.

■ HOPE, in Holland, Michigan, is another that merits a lot
more attention than it gets, raising higher education's moral
and intellectual levels. It is a place where parents can send
children of a wide range of abilities, knowing that their talents will be increased, their visions broadened, their ethical

acuities sharpened, and they will be prepared to prosper in a changed and changing world.

■ JUNIATA. I had long known Juniata, in rural central Pennsylvania, as a prolific producer of the nation's scientists and scholars before I paid a visit. Along with a strong sense of community, it has 100 percent medical acceptances, and nearly that in other health fields, including veterinary school. A model for getting women involved in health fields, it also gets a lot of science grants. An alumnus, Dr. William Phillips, was corecipient of the 1997 Nobel Prize in physics. Another, Dr. Williams von Liebig, was inventor of the Dacron tubing used in heart and blood vessel replacement. Other graduates are distinguished in several other fields. Every year the college has Mountain Day, an unannounced date when the school closes down and everybody goes to a nearby park for fun and games. At Christmas Madrigal Dinner, the faculty and administrators wait on the students.

■ KALAMAZOO, in that Michigan city, is more than a distinctive college; it is unique. No other college has its combination of a career development internship term, two foreign study terms, and a senior individualized project. The sense of community is strong because everybody eats together in the big dining hall, often with faculty members, to hear the excited reports of foreign study returnees; they also share joyous occasions and offer comfort on sorrowful ones. Kalamazoo's program appeals to the adventurous spirit and the inquiring mind; the timid learn by example to become risk-takers. A Kalamazoo graduate wrote on her commencement invitation, "Loren. Kalamazoo really did change my life!"

■ Knox, in Galesburg, Illinois, has a campus of great charm and tranquillity, of lovely lawns and great trees, and boasts the quintessential Old Main. The scene of a Lincoln-Douglas debate, it is a charming place to spend four important years of your life. But the cloistered scene is deceptive; Knox is a place of great intellectual ferment, and it has a new plan. The student must plan his own curriculum, and he must be able to work and communicate with people from a wide range of backgrounds. The plan was developed with the aid of a $200,000 Mellon Foundation grant and is likely to influence other colleges in this day of foreign study and a global world. The student, in designing his own program, must include a broad foundation in the liberal arts, experiential learning, independent research, write and speak well, and use information technology effectively, among other things. The plan is new and different, and the Knox graduates will be well prepared for a new millennium.

■ Lawrence, in Appleton, Wisconsin, like many others in this chapter, would be one of the prestigious few if it were in the Northeast. Harvard, Brown, and Duke have raided it for presidents. One of them, Nathan Pusey, developed Lawrence's powerful and much acclaimed Freshman Studies Program before Harvard snatched him.

■ Lynchburg is a college with a mission: minorities. It is on a beautiful campus of 214 acres, complete with lake and a Blue Ridge Mountain view, and it has had a rebirth. It develops talents and produces productive citizens with special emphasis on minorities, because it won't be many decades before WASPs are in the minority.

■ MARLBORO, on what was once a farm near Brattleboro, Vermont, has a little over three hundred students and is one of the most intellectually demanding colleges in the country, infinitely more so than any prestigious college or university. Although it was founded in 1946, it already is in the top four producers of future PhDs in the life sciences, along with Caltech, Chicago, and Reed.

■ MCDANIEL, in Westminster, Maryland, is an exceptional place; standards are high, grading tough, and English comp essays are graded by two instructors other than the assigning one. Seniors also score higher on some graduate exams, such as MCAT, than those at several Ivies. Their Ten Years Later testimonials show they wouldn't want it any other way; several hated to leave.

■ MILLSAPS is a pearl of great worth in an unlikely place, Jackson, Mississippi. It required an act of will for a hard-core integrationist to visit, but the rewards were great. It is a wonderful school, producing people with an acute sense of responsibility to society and a desire to serve. Among its many assets is a four-thousand-acre all-purpose laboratory in Yucatan, a forest preserve with two Mayan ruins. As the college says, "no discipline is left behind"; whatever her major, every student profits.

■ NEW, the honors college of the Florida state university system, has no required courses and an evaluation-based grading system, and produces winners wholesale. Along with Reed, Marlboro, St. John's, and Caltech, it is one of the five most intellectually challenging schools in the country, and its seven hundred students love it.

■ OHIO WESLEYAN, one of the best academic bargains in the country, is one of the top fifty producers of scientists. It is also one of the few liberal arts colleges that has a 3–2 program with Caltech. A chemistry professor expressed a prevailing faculty attitude when he said, "Regardless of where a kid comes from, we can take him somewhere."

■ REED, in Portland, Oregon, is for the teenager who's a genuine intellectual, lives the life of the mind, and wants to learn for the sake of learning. It has a beautiful campus and a very hardworking student body whose members go on to become winners at an unmatched rate. Reed is self-selective.

■ RHODES, in Memphis, Tennessee, has an elegant, Oxford-like campus of lovely grounds and many collegiate Gothic buildings. Every stone of them came from the same quarry, and every aspect of the college matches the beauty of the buildings and grounds.

■ ST. ANDREWS PRESBYTERIAN, in Laurinburg, North Carolina, was in the 2000 version of *Colleges That Change Lives*, but was taken out of the 2006 edition (after much agonizing) because it had been put on probation for financial reasons. The probation matter had not been settled by early 2007, but St. Andrews has done so much for several of my clients that I want to recognize its quality. St. Andrews was born in 1970 and is the only campus—six hundred acres with a seventy-acre lake in the middle—designed to give full access to kids with physical disabilities. Nearly 5 percent have some disability or are in wheelchairs. Some are millionaires as the result of auto accidents. St. Andrews has both National Merit Scholars and C and C– students. It has an honors program and plenty of TLC. St. Andrews has nearly eight hundred students, happy ones.

■ St. John's is one of the four most intellectual colleges in the country, along with Marlboro, New, and Reed. It has no majors or electives, one mission, two campuses, two presidents, two faculties, and two student bodies that move freely from the Annapolis to the Santa Fe campus, or vice versa. It is for the life-of-the-mind, learn-for-the-sake-of-learning person, but it is not stuffy about SATs or selective. As former dean Eva Brann said, "We're about as selective as a pickup baseball team. All we want is kids who read and can do a little mathematics."

■ St. Olaf, in Northfield, Minnesota, which is also home to Carleton, has a beautiful hilltop campus that makes one think of Camelot. It also has few equals in the many ways it ranks in the top tier of colleges academically. Its light and airy $29 million student center has been called a model for the twenty-first century. Its mailboxes have no locks; the students wanted it that way. When I was there in the early 1990s, several mailboxes in the former center were standing open, one with flowers, apparently for a girlfriend. St. Olaf is one of the few colleges in the country to offer majors in all four areas of the fine arts.

■ SOUTHWESTERN, in Georgetown, Texas, had a rebirth in the 1990s from a vocationally oriented place to a first-rate liberal arts college under President Roy B. Shilling, who brought in a first-rate young faculty and raised foundation funds for several new programs and facilities. In 2000 he was succeeded by Dr. Jake B. Shrum, the first alumni president, who has raised funds for a distinctive honors program, the Padeia Program. In 1994 Phi Beta Kappa, the scholastic honors society, gave Southwestern the stamp of approval by installing a chapter there. Now it is one of the few jewels of the Southwest, its mission to prepare the leaders for the new millennium.

■ URSINUS, in Collegeville, Pennsylvania, is a school that, like Southwestern, has had a rebirth as a first-rate liberal arts college, thanks to president John Strassburger (a former dean at Knox) and a faculty that shared the same vision. Since I visited in the 1990s, new majors have been added in dance, theater, art, American studies, and neuroscience, and an elaborate $25 million performing arts center opened in 2005. The faculty members talk like proud parents, and every kid I asked said they'd want their own to come to Ursinus. It has become a great school.

■ WABASH, in Crawfordsville, Indiana, is a happy band of 850 brothers, like no other college in the country. No student I talked to would be anywhere else. There simply is no better four years; the place produces a kind of religious bond, not to mention outstanding achievers in almost any field you want to name.

■ WHEATON, in the Chicago suburb of the same name, is the only college in this group that requires students to be Christians—liberal, evangelical, or anywhere in between. Wheaton has produced so many outstanding scholars, scientists, and other contributors to our society that it should be in any list of colleges that change lives. It is a happy place, even happier since the ban on dancing was lifted just before the new millennium.

■ WHITMAN, in Walla Walla, Washington, in addition to being a great school where faculty and students are intramural teammates and hiking companions, is a wonderful place for outdoorsy recreation and sports. This book has helped it become selective, but there are two alternatives for the outdoorsman or woman: Hendrix and Allegheny.

■ WOOSTER, in the Ohio town of the same name, has an unmatched record of turning out scholars, scientists, CEOs, and university presidents, among other distinctions, such as doubling the talents of a range of students. It is a community of learning that engenders great devotion.

More Superior Schools

■ COE COLLEGE, in Cedar Rapids, Iowa, is a school that has traditionally been strong in the sciences and today has three-fourths of its physics majors in graduate school, along with half its chemistry majors and 40 percent of its psychology majors going to graduate school. Its physics department is famed for its work in glass. The faculty take pride in their young charges, and the four years there are a transforming experience. Coe is also one of the Associated Colleges of the Midwest, one of the most forward-looking consortia in the nation. It has an outdoor classroom in its four-and-a-half-million-acre wilderness field station, where students can study the animals and plants of the Minnesota boundary waters. This learning community has an impact on its students way beyond graduate school. Over 98 percent of its 2006 graduates were in graduate school or had jobs in 2007.

■ COLLEGE OF THE ATLANTIC, in Bar Harbor, Maine, has been an overlooked bargain, partly because it is so small, with about three hundred students. A strong liberal arts college with an emphasis, as its name suggests, on the ocean, it is well worth looking at, but the looker should be socially sufficient enough to be happy in a small community.

■ GREEN MOUNTAIN COLLEGE, in Poultney, Vermont, is a good liberal arts college with an environmental emphasis, well worth investigating.

■ NORTHLAND COLLEGE, in Ashland, Wisconsin, is a committed liberal arts college with particular emphasis on the environment, for which its location on the south shore of Lake Superior is ideal. It accepts about 70 percent of its applicants, the great majority of whom are on financial aid. In this high-quality community of learning, you can major in many things that a more urban college wouldn't offer, as well as subjects like physics or history. The college weaves ecological and environmental subjects into the traditional liberal arts curriculum.

■ NORTH CENTRAL, in Naperville, Illinois, is a traditional liberal arts college of about 2,500 students in a Chicago suburb with an excellent faculty.

■ LUTHER COLLEGE, in Decorah, Iowa, has been a prolific producer of good citizens and outstanding people.

Afterword (Read It!)

I rest my case by reproducing the text of a now yellowed and brittle clipping torn out of the *Chronicle of Higher Education* way back in 1982. The fact that the article was written not by an educator but by the Omaha, Nebraska, owner of a scrap-metal business attests to its real-world validity. It has the stamp of universality; what he says applies with equal force to those who would be doctors, lawyers, engineers, scientists, or financial or industrial magnates. Its message was as true in 1982 as it was in 1882 or 1782 (witness Benjamin Franklin and Thomas Jefferson, American's first Renaissance men), and it will be recognized doctrine in the no-holds-barred, entrepreneurial world of 2022, for this maverick businessman's ideas are eternal verities.

Such other evidence in the book as the Haverford and Oberlin College and University of Virginia alumni surveys give consumer testimony to the value of a liberal education in fields far removed from their majors. This, from the venture capitalist employer's side, offers pungent proof that the life-giving message for everyone thinking about college is that what counts is empowerment of abilities and character. Neither the choice of major nor the name of the college, things that so concern you now, will make much difference. The *Chronicle*, the highly respected academic news journal, has never published a more cogent argument from any professor, provost, or president.

LIBERAL ARTS MAJORS PROVE SPECIALIZATION ISN'T REQUIRED FOR SUCCESS IN BUSINESS

By Sam Bittner

I have owned a scrap-metal business for 35 years. A year ago, I hired a new manager with unusual qualifications. He has an educational background of history and English; he holds a master's degree in foreign languages, and he speaks French and German fluently.

He knew nothing abut the scrap-metal business. I gave him one week of instruction, and told him to make mistakes and then use intelligence, imagination, and logic. He has turned this into one of the most efficiently run metal industries in the Middle West.

My company took a contract to extract beryllium from a mine in Arizona. I called in several consulting engineers and asked, "Can you furnish a chemical or electrolytical process that can be used at the mine site to refine directly from the ore?" Back came a report saying I was asking for

the impossible—a search of the computer tapes had
indicated that no such process existed.

I paid the engineers for their report. Then I hired a
student from Stanford University who was home for the
summer. He was majoring in Latin American history with
a minor in philosophy.

I gave him an airplane and a credit card and told
him, "Go to Denver and research the Bureau of Mines
archives and locate a chemical process for the recovery of
beryllium." He left on Monday. I forgot to tell him that I
was sending him for the impossible.

He came back on Friday. He handed me a pack of
notes and booklets and said, "Here is the process. It
was developed 33 years ago at a government research
station at Rolla, Mo." He then continued, "And here
also are other processes for the recovery of mica,
strontium, columbium, and yttrium, which also exist
as residual ores that contain beryllium." After one week of
research he was making sounds like metallurgical expert.

He is now back in school, but I am keeping track of
him. When other companies are interviewing the
engineering and the business-administration mechanics, I'll
be there looking for that history-and-philosophy major.*

During the past year, I, like every other business man,
was looking for new sources of financing because of the
credit crunch created by the interest market. I located my

---

* The history and philosophy major did not go into the scrap-metal business. After a research sojourn to Colombia during which a town's history that
he wrote became a television documentary, he is getting a PhD in filmmaking
at UCLA. But, Mr. Bittner reports, he's planning to make the scrap-metal company the subject of a film.

new sources. I simply hired a journalism student and gave him an assignment to write a report titled, "The Availability of Money and Credit in the United States."

These few examples represent simple solutions to business problems—solutions that require nothing more than the use of free, unrestrained intelligence and imagination.

It is unfortunate that our business world has become so structured that it demands specialization to such a degree that young people feel the need to learn only specific trades. By getting that type of education they hope to be able to find their way into one of those corporate niches.

If we continue with the present trend of specialized education, we are going to be successful in keeping a steady supply of drones moving to a large beehive. Our country was not built by a bunch of drones. It was built by people.

Have we lost sight of the fact that people are the most important commodity we have? They are not a collection of drones. They are individuals—each with intelligence, imagination, curiosity, impulses, emotions, and ingenuity.

In my business I want people who have those intangible qualities. Anyone can meet them. They are marching across the pages of books—poetry, history, and novels.

My hope is that in the process of choosing a college to make your future fruitful, these thoughts will help you precipitate out the sludge and produce a clear, unmuddled solution. Good luck!

Index

INDEX 267